Lex Fullarton & Dale Pinto

# Tax Accounting and Livestock in Australia

Insights from the *Wade Case*

T0343652

Lex Fullarton & Dale Pinto

# TAX ACCOUNTING AND LIVESTOCK IN AUSTRALIA

## Insights from the *Wade Case*

## Bibliografische Information der Deutschen Nationalbibliothek

Die Deutsche Nationalbibliothek verzeichnet diese Publikation in der Deutschen Nationalbibliografie; detaillierte bibliografische Daten sind im Internet über http://dnb.d-nb.de abrufbar.

## Bibliographic information published by the Deutsche Nationalbibliothek

Die Deutsche Nationalbibliothek lists this publication in the Deutsche Nationalbibliografie; detailed bibliographic data are available in the Internet at http://dnb.d-nb.de.

ISBN-13: 978-3-8382-1905-9

© *ibidem*-Verlag, Stuttgart 2024

Alle Rechte vorbehalten

Printed in the EU

# Table of Contents

**PART IV**
**AUSTRALIAN TAXATION OFFICE PRONOUNCEMENTS:**
**WHY TAX ADVISERS NEED TO EXERCISE CAUTION**

# Acknowledgements

Fullarton acknowledges his good friend, and early business partner, Alan Mc Kinnon. Mc Kinnon's tragic circumstances brought about this investigation into the tax treatment of Australian livestock. The book also acknowledges the long-term contribution to the Gascoyne pastoral industry and the sustainability research required to restore the natural environment of the arid shrublands of Western Australia, and in particular the SandRidge Gidgee country south of Carnarvon where Fullarton grew up, that is the research of the late John Charles Craig of Marron Station.

The authors acknowledge the work of Dr Narrelle Morris, Deputy Dean of Curtin Law School, Dr Peter Mellor, Adjunct Research Fellow at the Monash University, as well as the librarians at Curtin University, the University of Western Australia and the University of Notre Dame in sourcing records and material up to 70 years old. Further, the contributions made by Chris Wallis, barrister at law, and Dr John McLaren, senior lecturer in law, in arguing the finer details of this research is greatly appreciated.

The authors further acknowledge that the sections Tax Accounting for Livestock: Mother or Meat/Capital or Revenue? and The *Wade Case*: An analysis, were first published by Thomson Reuters New Zealand in the New Zealand Journal of Taxation Law and Policy volume 27 issue 1 March 2021 and issue 2 June 2021 respectively. For all subscription inquiries to that journal please phone, from New Zealand: 0800 10 60 60; from Overseas: +64 4 801 0001; or email:
Care.ANZ@thomsonreuters.com.

This book acknowledges all of those fighting in the Great Outback for their daily bread and to put food on the plates of the Nation and the World in general. The divide between rural and urban dwellers has contributed in no small way to the lack of appreciation of the difficulties faced by farmers, graziers and pastoralists on a daily basis. Along with the tyranny of distance, droughts, floods, fires, pestilences, heat, dust and taxes add to the daily struggle in the sunburnt country of the sweeping plains of the Great Outback (apologies to Dorothea Mackellar). It reveals part of their struggle. In particular it appreciates and acknowledges the people who took part in the survey which supports this research. It is through their insights that this book tells its story.

Finally, it would be quite wrong not to recognise the ongoing input and support from Mrs Julie Fullarton who is the eternal springboard of support and ideas which form the foundation of these writings and publications. Her special insight into the sociological influences of the people involved in this research is invaluable.

# Abbreviations

| | |
|---|---|
| AASB | Australian Accounting Standards Board |
| ABS | Australian Bureau of Statistics |
| AC | Law Reports, Appeal Cases (UK) |
| All ER | All England Law Reports |
| ATD | Australian Tax Decisions |
| ATO | Australian Taxation Office |
| ATP | Australian Tax Handbook |
| CGT | Capital Gains Tax |
| CLR | Commonwealth Law Reports (Aust) |
| CPA | Certified Practising Accountant |
| CTBR | Commonwealth Taxation Board of Review |
| CTBR(NS) | Commonwealth Taxation Board of Review (New Series) |
| Cth | Commonwealth of Australia |
| HCA | High Court of Australia |
| KBD | King's Bench Division (UK) |
| LR QB | Law Reports, Queens Bench Division (UK) |
| NSW | New South Wales |
| NZ | New Zealand |
| NZJTLP | New Zealand Journal of Taxation Law and Policy |
| IAS | International Accounting Standards Board |
| IASB | International Accounting Standards Board |
| IPA | Institute of Public Accountants |
| ITAA 1997 | Income Tax Assessment Act 1997 (Cth) |
| ITAA 1936 | Income Tax Assessment Act 1936 (Cth) |
| ITAA 1922 | Income Tax Assessment Act 1922 (Cth) |
| SAC | Statement of Accounting Concepts |
| SC | Supreme Court (UK) |
| TBRD | Taxation Board of Review Decision |
| TC | Official Tax Case Reports (UK) |
| TLR | Times Law Reports (UK) |
| UK | United Kingdom |
| UKHL | House of Lord (UK) |
| WA | Western Australia |

# Preface

*Central to the background and motivation for the publication of this book, and the others in a series written by Lex Fullarton, is his family history and personal background of being born and raised in the Northwest of Western Australia. He was born in Carnarvon in 1956 and raised there, except for a short period in Broome, in the early 1960s. He was the only child of Kathy Collins and Bob Fullarton who were married there in 1952.*

*His Mother's family were old pastoral station folk. From an early age he and his father wandered the Bush around Carnarvon fishing and shooting. The small family was not wealthy but very resilient and able to do quite a lot with very little. In that physical and social environment, he developed an eclectic range of social experiences and appreciation of the natural environment is the sensitive desert environment of the Gascoyne region. He spent his school holidays Jackerooing on friends' sheep stations.*

*Three important factors arose from that. He learned to be resilient by living and work in the Bush, fencing, maintaining wells and windmills, and handling stock; He learned the practical application of education; and developed a thirst for experimentation. It is against that background these books are written.*

*This book is the fifth in that series which focus on taxation issues in Outback Western Australia. They look at how taxation influences social, economic and environmental development in Australia from a range of aspects.*

*The first book, 'Heat, Dust and Taxes' (2015), told the story of how tax avoidance schemes were mass-marketed in the 1990s and how the blue-collar workers in the Pilbara Region of Western Australia eagerly participated in them. As with many get rich quick schemes in history they came to an abrupt end with the usual grief, both economic and social, levelled on the unwary victims. Fullarton had firsthand experience of the aftermath as a tax practitioner in the North West of Western Australia.*

*The second book 'Watts in the Desert' (2016), covered the history of the first privately owned, commercial solar farm in Australia that Fullarton and his family constructed from a long-abandoned camel holding paddock on the outskirts of Carnarvon. In it he traced the history of the land from British Colonisation when Fullarton's ancestors arrived in the region in 1883, to the development of the solar farm and the integration of an ice-works to demonstrate and 'alternative use for alternative energy' in 2009 and a trial of incorporating of wind turbines into the solar farm's renewable energy system. It also described how Australia's renewable energy legislation functions to provide a taxation and subsidisation scheme to promote the growth of renewable energy in Australia at the expense of the fossil-fuelled energy industry.*

*The third book 'The Artful Aussie Tax Dodger' (2017), focussed primarily on the history of income tax in Australia from 1915, with the introduction of the Commonwealth Income Tax Assessment Act 1915, to its centenary in 2015. It looked broadly at some of the methods taxpayers have used in Australia to avoid tax such as the use of trusts which have been used as tax avoidance structures from medieval times in Britain to complex trust structures used by high wealth individuals in the modern age. It critically analysed tax avoidance schemes in Australia that extend to offshore tax havens and other such schemes. It also looked at Australia's consumption tax which was introduced in 2000, Goods and Services Tax (GST). It examined the 'regressivity' of the tax, that is how it impacts lower income earners harder than high income earners, and traced the political history of its origins as well as comparing it to the then South Pacific Island tax haven of the Cook Islands Value Added Tax (VAT). Finally, it examined the issue of tax reform in Australia and looked at some of the reviews of the taxation system commissioned by the Federal Parliament from the Asprey Report of 1975 to the Ralph Report of 2009.*

*[T]Axing Greenhouse Gases (2019) gave a detailed comparison of Australia's carbon taxes between the Renewable Energy (Electricity) Act of 2000 and the short-lived Clean Energy Act of 2011. It provided a method for accounting for the creation, sale, purchase and surrender of carbon credits in the hands of renewable energy generating enterprises and electricity generators which use fossil fuelled energy sources. It also examined the taxation impacts of the introduction of electric vehicles of Australian*

*roads and the transition away from petroleum based internal combustion engines.*

*The common thread throughout this series is how taxation* systems *can play a significant role in combatting global atmospheric warming due to air pollution. It cannot go unnoticed that Australia is experiencing cataclysmic weather events largely due to rising atmospheric temperatures caused by greenhouse gas emissions – climate change. The authors hope that these books can go some way to allaying social and political fears that taxes and the transition away from the dependence on polluting fossil fuels to a cleaner and even more productive future. The economy need not suffer and social issues are cared for while cleaning up the natural environment.*

*The impacts of the Covid Pandemic have held up the publication of this book until now. However, Professor Dale Pinto of the Curtin Law School has come on board with the development of this book which looks specifically at the taxation issues affecting Australian primary producers on the sale of their properties. It is particularly noted that some of the sales are forced upon farmers and graziers for a raft of personal reasons as well as the disasters visited upon then by nature. It is also noted that global warming is increasing the frequency and harshness of those events. The writing of this book was influenced by one such disaster experienced by one family in Outback Western Australia. Once again Fullarton's personal experience and family history has provided background to the subject.*

# List of Figures

# List of Colour Plates

# List of Tables

# Chapter One
# Overview

## 1.1 Overview

The maps below show the Pastoral and Wheat-sheep farming zones and the population distribution in Australia. While the regions are vast and occupy most of the continent, they are sparsely populated and the majority of Australians reside in the towns and cities in the high rainfall zone along the east coast and south west of Western Australia.

The research reveals there were limited numbers of taxpayers, tax accountants and others associated with pastoral land sales in the broader Australian population. The sparsity of population in the regions and the limited number of annual sales of such properties may go some way to explaining why there was some difficulty in finding people familiar with the topic of this book.

Generally urban tax professionals and accountants followed the Australian Tax Office (ATO) advice without further investigation. The final part of this book caveats against reliance on ATO pronouncements without conducting due diligence in the preparation of income tax returns for and on behalf of taxpayers.

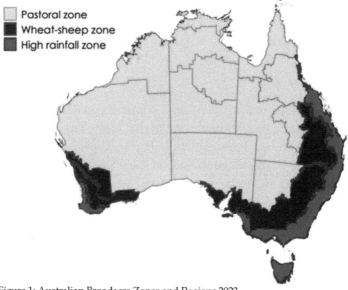

Figure 1: Australian Broadacre Zones and Regions 2023.
(Courtesy Australian Government, Department of Agriculture, Fisheries and Forestry)

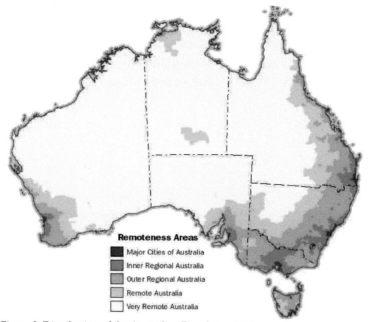

Figure 2: Distribution of the Australian Population 2023.
(Courtesy Australian Government, Australian Bureau of Statistics)

This book considers the disposal of animals held in a business of primary production in conjunction with the sale of a farm or pastoral lease. In the normal conduct of the business those animals might not be sold but as a consequence of droughts, floods, fires, tempests and family disasters is the sale or loss of valuable stud stock. In normal trading circumstances, these animals would not be sold as trading stock. However, the sale of pastoral properties can be beyond the will of the owners for a raft of reasons. The ATO view is that the revenue from the sale of ALL animals sold as part of a primary production business is income according to ordinary concepts and the receipts are taxed as ordinary income.

That view deprives owners of a raft of tax concessions granted to other business owners on the sale of their businesses. The authors consider this situation to be grossly unfair to pastoralists, farmers and graziers who are forced to sell their breeding stock due to natural disasters or along with their businesses on retirement from the industry.

This book looks at how the view was established and why it came into being. It looks at the basis on which the ATO formed its view and examines the litigation which the ATO uses to support its opinion - Federal Commissioner of Taxation v Wade (Wade Case)'.[1] It then examines the background of the *Wade Case* in detail and court documents presented in the preceding trial and administrative reviews.

It finds that their Honours were obliged to accept the principal that ALL animals held in a business of primary production are to be considered livestock, and therefore revenue assets rather than capital assets — regardless of the role they play in the business. It notes that one of the three judges expressed concern in accepting that principal.

Finally, the book examines legislative amendments to the Australian tax legislation in 1936. Those amendments prevent livestock from being considered as capital in a business of primary production in Australia. It suggests those amendments were made by a mistake by the Australian Parliament in its reaction to

---

1    *Federal Commissioner of Taxation v Wade* (1951) 84 CLR 105 (*'Wade Case'*).

recommendations contained in of the Ferguson Royal Commission on Taxation 1934.[2]

It suggests that the doubts that Kitto J expressed in the *Wade Case* may well be justified and that reliance on that litigation might not be a sound basis to form the opinion held by the ATO. It then cautions that ATO announcements and published views should not be relied on solely as support for advice given by tax lawyers and professionals to taxpayers. It notes that most ATO advice carries a caveat to that effect and advises taxpayers to seek independent legal advice when interpreting tax law in Australia.

The book notes that a pervious case which was very similar to the *Wade Case* of 1951, the Robinson Case of 1927[3] decided the opposite of decision handed down in Wade. Therefore, this book investigates matters beyond the *Wade Case* and finds the critical tax legislation was amended in 1936.

Intuitively the authors set out to find why cases relating to the same issue — that of stud stock or animals kept for their product rather than for trade were different. The book discovered that section 17 of the Income Tax Assessment Act 1922 (ITAA 1922) had been repealed from its successor, the Income Tax Assessment Act 1936 (ITAA 1936). That section provided for an election to be made as to whether animals could be treated as capital assets or revenue assets. The removal of that provision thereafter compels taxpayers to consider ALL animals held in a business of primary production to be revenue assets regardless of the role they play in the business.

This book concludes that the basis for the repeal was a mistake and that Parliament amended the legislation based on a mistake of interpretation of the recommendations made in the Ferguson Royal Commission on Taxation report of 1934.[4] It recommends that Parliament be made aware of the mistake and that s 17 be re-enacted to correct an anomaly in Australia's current tax legislation which

---

2    Commonwealth, *Royal Commission on Taxation* (1932-34) (Ferguson Royal Commission Report).
3    *Robinson v Federal Commissioner of Taxation* [1927] HCA 8; (1927) 39 CLR 297 ('Robinson Case').
4    Commonwealth, *Royal Commission on Taxation* (Third Report, 12 April 1934) (Ferguson Report).

prevents retiring pastoralists, farmers and graziers from benefitting from tax concessions available to other business owners on their retirement.

As with the previous books, the framework of the research design is a mixed methods research approach that has been adopted to support the book's findings, conclusions and recommendations.[5]

## 1.2 Structure

The book moves from the broad to the specific in four parts. Each part has been published in a peer-reviewed academic journal to provide rigor and reader confidence in the conclusions and recommendations of the book. The parts move from the broad topic of tax accounting for livestock in Australia to a detailed examination of the litigation supporting the ATO view and finally a caveat to tax professionals practice of accepting ATO opinions without challenge.

PART I    Tax Accounting for Livestock;
PART II   The *Wade Case;*
PART III  The Foundations of the *Wade Case;* and
PART IV   Australian Taxation Office Pronouncements.

Figure 3 shows the how the sections relate to each other and illustrates how the research investigations developed to reach the final conclusions.

---

5    John Ward Cresswell, *Research Design: Qualitative, Quantitative and Mixed Methods Approaches* (2nd ed, 2003) 18.

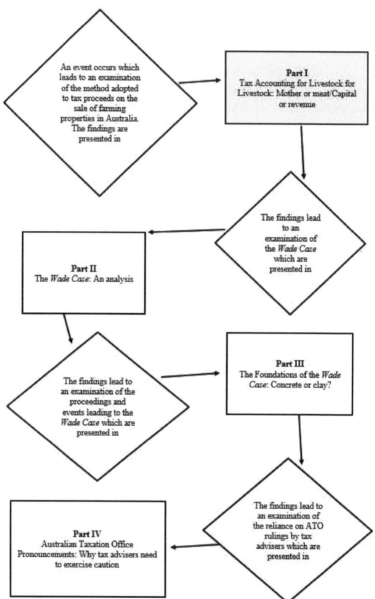

Figure 3: Flowchart of the research.

## 1.3 Section Outlines

### PART I Tax Accounting for Livestock for Livestock: Mother or meat/Capital or revenue

This part looks at the sale of rural properties in Australia and considers the value of animals included in the sale of those properties. It argues that the provisions of the Income Tax Assessment Act 1997 are being misinterpreted by tax administrators and tax professionals. By considering the sale of ALL animals traded during the sale of a pastoral lease or farm as revenue vendors are denied tax concessions which are permitted under the capital gains tax provisions of the Australian Income Tax Assessment Act.

The research reveals that the ATO view, that all animals held in a primary production business are considered to the trading stock regardless of the function they perform and duration they are held, relied entirely on the decision held in the *Wade Case* of 1951. That perspective led to further research into the decision handed down in that case. Part II is the presentation of the findings of that research.

### PART II The *Wade Case*: An analysis

Part I examines the background and reasons why the ATO established its view on the tax accounting treatment of livestock in a business of primary production. It finds that the primary basis for that view is the decision of the *Wade Case*. Therefore, Part II examines the *Wade Case* in detail to establish *why* their Honours reached their decisions.

Part II finds that their Honours accepted the concept that ALL animals held in a business of primary production were considered trading stock regardless of the function that they perform in the operation of the business as a matter of the operation of the Law. No further investigation was made by them as to why that was so. It concludes that the *Wade Case* was primarily a decision as to the assessablilty of monies paid to a taxpayer as insurance recoveries for loss and replacement of assets. It was immaterial as to the class of asset. Therefore, the concept of livestock being capital or revenue assets had no real impact on the final decision of the Court.

Critically, it is noted that Kitto J expressed reservations that dairy cattle could be considered as trading stock, but as the matter was primarily focussed on the assessablilty of insurance payments that factor was immaterial to the case. PART II also finds other cases, which focused on the distinction between livestock as capital or revenue assets, such as the *Robinson Case*, had decided that livestock could be considered as capital assets. It concludes that the reliance by the ATO on the *Wade Case* might be successfully challenged.

To investigate further as to why the decisions of the two cases differed a further investigation was conducted into the background of the *Wade Case* to establish what may have happened between 1927 and 1951 to make such a significant difference in the outcomes of what where otherwise two very similar cases. The matter that *Robinson* focussed on sheep and *Wade* focussed on dairy cattle is immaterial as both are livestock held for their produce and not for trade. The sheep being for wool and the cattle for milk. The findings of that research are continued in Part III.

**PART III The Foundations of the *Wade Case*: Concrete or clay?**

The research contained in Part III looked at why the **Robinson Case** of 1927 decided differently to the *Wade Case* of 1951. It was found that Australia's income tax legislation had been reviewed in 1934[6] and that a critical piece of legislation that allowed the decision to consider some livestock as capital assets had been repealed in the *ITAA 1936*. This Part finds that it was the repeal of section 17 of the *Income Tax Assessment Act 1922* (ITAA 1922) the prevented primary producers from classifying some animals as livestock for trading, thereby making ALL animals held in a business of primary production trading stock and therefore revenue assets rather than capital assets.

---

6    Ferguson Royal Commission Report (n 2).

The Ferguson Royal Commission reported that pastoralists and graziers had been classifying their sheep as capital assets thereby avoiding income tax on the sale of their flocks. It reported that there was difficulty in segregating the value of the fleece, carried by the animal at sale, and the value of the sheep itself. The entire receipt on the sale was applied to the animal and nothing to the wool that it carried. Thus, tax was avoided on the 'income'.

It was recommended that for 'simplicity' the animal be classified as trading stock. The simplest solution was to repeal 17 and remove the option from the vendor.

Part III concludes that it is the repeal of s 17 from the ITAA 1922 such that the option was not carried forward to the new ITAA 1936. Therefore, the ATO view is correct, however not supported by the decision of the *Wade Case* but rather as a matter of legislation. It appears from the research that when Wade's income tax return was lodged in 1948 and subsequent series of appeals and reviews that none of the individuals dealing with the matter, including their Honours, were aware of the legislative amendment. The transcript of the decision in *Wade* notes that the classification was accepted by their honours, even though Kitto J expressed difficulty in accepting that the dairy cattle were not capital assets.

Fullarton has an advantage as to the classification of livestock in that he has a pastoral background and worked as a Jackeroo[7] on pastoral stations. He suggests simpler solution might have been to add a condition to the application of s 17 that for the option granted under s 17 to apply the sheep had to be shorn before sale. The term is called 'off shears'. It is interesting that in 1936, when Australia 'rode on the sheep's back' that the parliamentarians did not make that realisation. In fairness the Explanatory Memorandum which accompanied the Bill did not consider the option.

This book suggests that s 17, or an equivalent provision could be enacted to restore equity to the tax legislation and address the perceived tax avoidance method.

---

7    Junior pastoral station worker. Assumed to become a station manager rather than a station hand or general labourer.

Of significance to this book is that while the ATO view has been proven correct by the research findings, it is formed on a 'clay footing'. It might be that the findings of the *Wade Case* might be challenged rendering the advice unreliable. Part IV examines the dangers of relying solely on ATO pronouncements for the treatment of transactions for taxation purposes.

**PART IV Australian Taxation Office Pronouncements: Why tax advisers need to exercise caution**

The final part considers the modern ATO practice of issuing pronouncements of its view as to the treatment of transactions for taxation purposes. It suggests that in the modern environment of complex taxation law there is ever-evolving legislation and interpretation. To maintain the high professional standards that are ethically and legally required, tax practitioners are obliged to engage in close scrutiny of the law to obtain a clear understanding.

However, tax practitioners find it increasingly difficult to keep themselves informed while dealing with the pressures of their workloads. Therefore, to assist practitioners, professional bodies are constantly providing information and commentary about changes to statutory and case law. Further, ATO issues its own interpretations, rulings and other such proclamations, to guide taxpayers and practitioners and assist in compliance.

The authors' research suggests that the sometimes confusing and apparently convoluted legislative change and evolving case law are leading practitioners to become increasingly reliant on ATO rulings and advice rather than conducting their own legislative research and making their own interpretations of statutes.

It argues that the practice of accepting ATO opinions without challenge can have extremely significant fiscal impacts on taxpayers and tax collections. It warns that tax practitioners should not always consider that the rulings, determinations and advice provided by the ATO give the greater clarity and certainty in the preparation and lodgement of taxation returns and the payment of tax that are sought by practitioners.

# PART I

# TAX ACCOUNTING FOR LIVESTOCK: MOTHER OR MEAT/CAPITAL OR REVENUE?

*This part was first published as an article in the New Zealand Journal of Taxation Law and Policy in March 2021 27(1). It is re-published here mutatis mutandis with permission of the publisher.*

*It examines the current method of accounting for the sale of animals held in a business of primary production in Australia.*

# Chapter Two
# The Problem

## 2.1 Introduction

This part argues that the revenue from the sale of stud, or breeding, animals should be taxed under the capital gains tax (CGT) provisions of the Income Tax Assessment Act 1997 (ITAA 1997) and not as income according to ordinary concepts.

It examines the distinction between classifying expenditures by an enterprise as capital (assets purchased) or revenue (costs of operation). In particular, it looks at the taxation implications of accounting for livestock as trading stock purchased or bred for sale and those animals purchased or bred for breeding purposes. It considers the view of the ATO that ALL animals in a primary production business are considered trading stock, and the revenue from the sale is classified as income according to ordinary concepts and is therefore subject to income tax rates.

Figure 4 depicts a young shorthorn heifer. Is she destined to become a mother and therefore classified as a production animal (a capital asset), or produce (a revenue asset)? That issue is examined in this part as it argues that some animals should be classified as capital assets and therefore subject to the capital gains tax (CGT) provisions on their sale, instead of being classified as trading stock and subject to ordinary income tax rates.

Figure 4: A Young Heifer on the Rangelands of Western Australia.[8]

To illustrate the distinction, the mustering crew at De Grey Station in Western Australia is shown in Figure 5. It is fair to assume that the inclusion of the horse-mounted stockmen and women indicates the horses are part of the station plant and not livestock for trading purposes.

Figure 5: 'Meet the Crew' – the Mustering Team from De Grey Station.[9]

Another pastoral station manager stated that his horses and dogs were very expensive and highly trained. He said they had a key role

8   Photograph of "Outback Heifer" taken by Alexander Robert Fullarton (2020).
9   Photograph of "Meet the Crew", De Grey Station – Central Station, Central Station at <www.centralstation.net.au/>. (Reproduced by permission of Mark Bettini of De Grey Station).

in his mustering operations and could not be regarded as livestock in any way. 'To regard them as livestock is a lack of understanding of the pastoral industry.'[10] The illustrations are shown here to support the argument that ALL animals are not trading stock and that some should be regarded as capital assets.

This book argues that valuable stud animals are kept for breeding purposes and not for general sale as trading stock. Those animals are generally included in the sale of pastoral properties. Other than being sold with the properties, those animals are generally not sold as part of normal trading operations but may be sold at the end of their useful working life. Occasionally, sales of those animals may occur for other reasons such as droughts but not in the normal course of business.

To consider ALL animals as trading stock in Australia is not supported by the legislation. It is noted that the word ALL is not contained in s 995-1 of the ITAA 1997.

This book argues that the definition of livestock should not be extended to include animals held for their produce or used as working beasts. It suggests that the ATO's interpretation of livestock is too broad, and taxpayers are being deprived of CGT concessions and exemptions on the sale of pastoral properties in Australia. It is noted that the ATO view relies primarily on the findings in *Federal Commissioner of Taxation v Wade (Wade Case)'*.[11] The *Wade Case* is not examined in this part but rather in detail in the following Part II.

This part deals with the accounting perspective. Therefore, to provide background and context, an overarching accounting pillar — the principle of ownership of a trading entity — is considered. The accounting proprietorship equation is: Proprietorship (capital) is equal to Assets (what it owns) less Liabilities (what it owes) (P = A-L). It is understood that expenses reduce profits and therefore the value of a proprietorship, but the purchase of capital assets is a redistribution of profits and does not reduce but rather maintains the value of the proprietorship in a form other than cash.

---

10    Telephone Conversation with Sean D'Arcy, owner and manager of Lyndon Station, Western Australia (Alexander Robert Fullarton, Curtin Law School, Curtin University, 24 December 2019).

11    *Wade Case* (n 1).

Revenue generated from the sale of goods or services in the ordinary course of business generates profits that are subject to income tax according to ordinary concepts,[12] but funds received from the sale of assets are a realisation of assets and do not generate a trading profit. Hence, any change in the value of the asset held by an entity on realisation will create a capital gain or loss and is treated differently from trading profits for taxation purposes.[13]

An example is provided below to illustrate and acknowledge that some receipts from some sources and activities fall outside the definition of ordinary income,[14] and some receipts may not be considered income at all.

Revenue received by householders for electricity generated by small domestic solar photovoltaic (PV) systems is not considered as assessable income by the ATO. The ATO view is that those systems do not provide regular, reliable and realistic opportunities to profit from the arrangement, nor are they a "product of any employment, services rendered of business".[15] Therefore, income received from the sale of electricity to the grid is considered to be of a private or domestic nature and not income according to ordinary concepts.[16] It is also noted that the costs associated with the installation, depreciation and maintenance of the solar PV system are likewise not deductible.[17] Albeit outside the scope of this discussion, the example illustrates that the view that ALL income is assessable income may not be accurate. Therefore, the word ALL should be applied with caution.

It is argued that the sale of breeding stock is the sale of business assets, especially when in conjunction with the sale of a pastoral property. Therefore, revenue received from the sale is not trading income according to ordinary concepts but rather a capital gain,

---

12    Income Tax Assessment Act 1936 (Cth), s 25; and Income Tax Assessment Act 1997 (Cth), s 6-5 (ITAA 1997).
13    ITAA 1997, pt 3-1, div 100.
14    ITAA 1997, s 6-1(5).
15    Australian Taxation Office *Photovoltaic Solar System* (Private Ruling, Authorisation Number 1012329040193, November 2011, edited 2019).
16    Ibid.
17    Ibid.

and the funds should be taxed as a capital gain, not as ordinary income.

The argument is illustrated by a scenario that considers the sale of cattle in association with the sale of a pastoral lease. It looks at the beasts sold in conjunction with the sale of the pastoral business to consider

- Whether all animals on the property and sold as part of the transfer of the business should be considered as trading stock as part of the operation of the business, that is, revenue items and therefore taxed as income according to ordinary concepts; or
- Whether animals on the property retained for breeding purposes and not generally for sale as part of the day-to-day operations of the property should be considered as capital assets and therefore taxed as capital gains and entitled to the capital gains tax discounts and s 152-D exemptions.

This part considers how the proceeds from the sale of a cattle station allocated to the animals retained for breeding purposes should be treated by describing the funds as a capital gain or loss for accounting and taxation purposes. It contends that the sale of pastoral and similar properties terminates the operation of the business. Therefore, the proceeds are not income according to ordinary concepts (normal trading) but rather are income from the sale of assets or from the liquidation and cessation of one business and the commencement of another. The authors argue that the component of those animals used as aids in manufacturing to produce goods — either by way of breeding trade animals or animal produce such as dairy products — be treated as capital assets, not trading stock, as currently considered by the ATO.[18]

---

18  Letter from Alison Lendon, Deputy Commissioner of Taxation, to Alexander Robert Fullarton, 6 November 2019 (held by the author). The context is the ATO's view that all animals in a primary production business are considered as livestock within the definition of s 995-1 of the ITAA 1997. In the taxation advice letter provided to the author regarding the ATO's view of the classification of livestock in a primary production business, Lendon states, "The Commissioner [of Taxation] considers that the definition of livestock in section 995-

The ATO view is supported by its reference to "the majority ruling of Dixon and Fullagar JJ in the High Court decision" of the *Wade Case*.[19] However, it is argued that some livestock should be considered as aids to manufacturing, or as breeding stock (s 385-100).

To provide background and context, the book briefly considers the purchase or creation of assets.

To illustrate the importance of taxation relief from the classification of stud animals as capital assets, div 118 of the ITAA 1997 acts to prevent the imposition of dual taxation on one transaction. Division 118 of the ITAA 1997 prescribes exemptions to CGT if income tax has been applied to that transaction. An in-depth examination of div 118 is beyond the scope of this research, but the relevant subsections are briefly outlined to illustrate how they might be applied to this research.

Consideration is specifically given to:

- s 118-20, which prevents CGT provisions from applying to revenue that is classified as assessable income for income tax purposes — that is, both income tax and CGT cannot be levied on the same revenue from the same transaction;
- s 118-24, which deals with capital gains arising from the application of capital allowances created under div 40; and
- s 118-25, which prevents CGT provisions from applying to revenue received from the sale of trading stock — that is, for revenue generated from the sale of assets as in s 118-20 but specifically applied to trading stock.

To assist the reader, Figure 6 provides a decision matrix for the classification of goods into assets of a capital nature or products for resale to generate income or revenue. It shows the impact of segregating expenditures into revenue and capital and reveals the class of

---

1 of the Income Tax Assessment Act 1997 includes all animals in a primary production business."

19   Ibid.

tax applicable to income according to ordinary concepts and gains from the sale of capital assets.

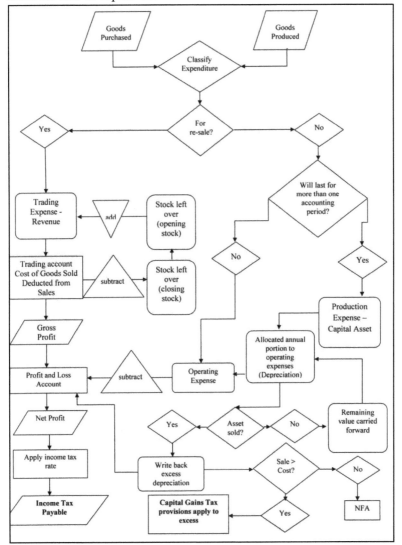

Figure 6: Decision Matrix to Reveal the Tax Impact of Determining Purchases as Expenses or Assets.

Kenny and Devos suggest that it is incumbent upon tax preparers and advisers to ensure capital gains tax (CGT) concessions are properly considered and reported. Hence, it is important for business owners, accountants and tax professionals to consider the classification of capital and revenue expenditure. It is also critical to consider the distinction between capital assets, which are subject to CGT, and transactions of a revenue nature, which are subject to income tax.

They state:

> Small business and/or their advisers will need to plan for the many [capital gains] tax concessions [available to small business entities in Australia]. Given the numerous concessions and the differing small business thresholds, this will impose significant costs for small business at or near any of the various thresholds.[20]

The principle of the case study supporting the findings of this book is that if the remaining cattle of any value are considered as breeding stock, then they are capital items. In such cases, CGT small business discounts apply, in particular the s 152-D exemption.

While the definition of livestock is contained within the provisions of the current income tax legislation (ITAA 1997), Lendon's advice[21] relies on the 69-year-old *Wade Case*.[22] There are several explanations as to why the issue has not been challenged in nearly three-quarters of a century.

Generally, the CGT concessions apply only to individuals, and the bulk of pastoral leases are operated by corporate structures. Therefore, this issue may be considered extremely insignificant in the broader scope of the tax administrators and preparers in Australia. In addition, individuals disposing of their properties are generally elderly and retiring from working life. They may not be inclined to engage in protracted disputes with the ATO at that point in their lives and simply accept the higher-than-necessary tax burden as just another imposition on farmers, which they have endured all of their farming lives.

---

20   Paul Kenny and Ken Devos *Australian Small Business Taxation* (Butterworths, 2018) 170.
21   Lendon (n 18).
22   (1951) 84 CLR 105.

The regions where the activities are conducted are generally in the remote arid regions of Australia. The factor of remoteness may have influenced the lack of scrutiny of this issue in modern taxation policy and administration. In addition to being conducted in remote regions, sales of pastoral leases are comparatively rare when compared to the overall number of other transfers of land.[23] In Western Australia, the average number of land transfers processed by the Western Australian Land Information Authority (Landgate) is about 5,700 per month.[24] As shown in Figure 7, there were merely 361 transfers of pastoral leases in Western Australia over the 38 years from 1980 to 2018.

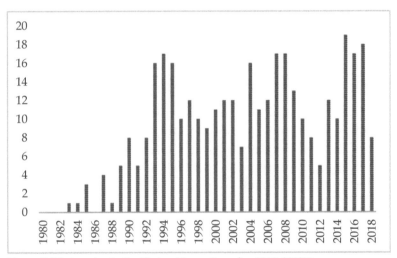

Figure 7: Western Australian Pastoral Lease Transfers 1980–2018.[25]

The modal average sale price is approximately A$1 million. That is not a significant sum when compared to a home in an Australian

23    Data provided by Government of Western Australia, Western Australian Land Information Authority ("Landgate") *Pastoral Lease Sales from 1980* (2019), advised by email from Greg Walker, Service Manager, Business & Government Solutions Strategy, Customers and Culture Landgate, to Alexander Robert Fullarton, 19 December 2019.

24    Government of Western Australia *Business Activity* (2019) <https://catalogue.d ata.wa.gov.au/>.

25    Government of Western Australia, Western Australian Land Information Authority (n 23).

city. In addition, just 10 sales per year is unlikely to raise concerns for taxation administrators.

Further, this book finds that tax preparers, pastoralists and their agents are somewhat divided in their opinions as to whether breeding animals, sold in conjunction with the transfer of pastoral properties, should be classified as capital or revenue assets. Those opinions are from persons involved in the modern pastoral industry and may differ from the view of the ATO, which is primarily based on a case that occurred in the dairy industry in Western Australia in the late 1940s.[26]

To cover the broad range of influencing factors identified, this book uses a mixed method research approach including:

- a series of interviews with stakeholders engaged in the operation and sale of pastoral properties in Western Australia who were asked to consider a hypothetical case study; and
- a quantitative survey using a Likert scale response system.

The following section outlines a hypothetical case study to provide background and context to the research. It outlines the case study put to the research participants for their consideration.

Although the scenario closely follows an actual event that is under scrutiny in this book, it is used to protect the privacy of the taxpayer concerned. In the close community of the pastoral region of Western Australia, some readers may identify the property, but all reasonable attempts have been made to disguise the actual persons involved. For ethical reasons, their permission has been obtained to publish redacted documents provided by them for the purposes of this research.

---

26    *Wade Case* (n 1).

# Chapter Three
# The Research

## 3.1 Hypothetical Case Study

A woman works hard at her trade in a city and decides that one day she will own a cattle spread. The reality is that all she can afford is a very run-down station in a very remote and arid area. It is marginal, but with hard work, and some luck, it might return a modest income.

After about 10 years of much sweat and toil, and more than a few drops of blood in the 'bulldust', she is making a go of it. The harsh environment slowly gives way to her persistent husbandry. She has built up a reasonable stock of breeders, purchased a couple of good quality bulls and managed to turn off a reasonable number of cattle for market. She has passed 40 years of age and her 50th birthday is not far away — but look at this! She is the boss of her very own cattle empire (well, small village, really). She is far from the levels of Sidney Kidman,[27] but she is living the dream, not the nightmare.

Disaster strikes! The persistent headaches, initially written off as due to lack of water and too much Fosters,[28] are diagnosed as symptoms of terminal brain cancer. She has a year, maybe two left, according to the medical practitioner. She has lived a hard life and dies with dignity.

The property is sold, and her estate distributed. In preparation for the sale, she had mustered the property and every beast of commercial value was stripped from the property and sold. Only the breeding stock and animals too light to cover the costs of sale are turned back onto the grazing land.

---

27  Sir Sidney Kidman, Australian Pastoralist, 1857–1935. Sidney Kidman left school at the age of 13 to become a cattleman in South Australia. He died, a cattle baron, in 1935.

28  An Australian brand of beer favoured by the people of the pastoral regions of Australia.

The breeders had to be kept to provide marketable beasts to be included in the sale of the property, and the 'weaners'[29] would not return a reasonable profit at the point of sale of the property, even though they might well grow and be saleable in the future. The property is marketed, sold and settled within six weeks of the final muster.

Upon investigation, the executor of her will finds that the opinion of a number of public accountants is that while the proceeds of the sale of the property are generally considered a capital gain, the revenue from the sale of the remaining cattle is considered as the sale of trading stock and therefore liable to income tax at personal income tax rates. They point to s 995 of the ITAA 1997 to justify their opinion.

The executor argues that the small animals turned off are below commercial trade weight. While they will become valuable in the future, at the point of sale they were of no commercial value. He further argues that the breeding stock kept back for breeding purposes are capital items as they are used to manufacture products for sale in the same way that a lathe is used to make machine parts for sale.

The key to the case is the matter of capital gains tax exemptions applicable to an individual taxpayer on the sale of a business forced by medical factors. The executor argues that as the owner was under 55 years of age, quite clearly ill and subsequently died, the revenue from the disposal of the property, including the animals, thereupon is a capital gains tax event and permitted to claim the applicable capital gains tax exemptions.

The dominant theme of this research is to provide an understanding of the distinction between capital and revenue for accounting and taxation purposes. The focus of this study is the significance of the distinction between fixed and current assets because increases in the value of capital (capital gains) and profits from trading (revenue) are treated quite differently for taxation purposes.

---

29   Young animals recently weaned from their mothers as part of normal farming practice, particularly calves and lambs.

Under Australian tax law, the sale of current assets is likely to fall under the income tax provisions of the ITAA 1997. Profits arising from the sale are taxed as income according to ordinary concepts, and income tax rates are imposed on them. In contrast, the sale of fixed assets is more likely to fall under the capital gains tax provisions of the ITAA 1997. Profits arising from the sale may be taxed as capital gains and may be taxed at a different rate and/or subject to a raft of discounts and exemptions.

It is noted here that this issue appears to apply only in Australia. Unlike the Australian legislation, the New Zealand legislation specifically includes ALL livestock as trading stock.[30] The New Zealand Inland Revenue Department has issued a public ruling to that effect under s 91D of the Tax Administration Act 1994 (NZ).[31]

In Australia, income tax rates are substantially higher than capital gains tax rates. Prior to 1985, the imposition of tax on income from capital gains was very limited,[32] and often, shifting profits from revenue income to capital gains receipts was used as a method of tax arbitrage.[33]

Section 3 considers the distinction between capital and revenue expenditures from both accounting and legal perspectives. It looks at the basic accounting conventions of proprietorships, or the owner's investment in an enterprise; capital purchases (long-term assets); and revenue purchases (trading expenses). It also reviews cases that have considered the distinction between proceeds from

---

30    Income Tax Act 2007 (NZ), s YA 1: (definition of 'trading stock').
31    New Zealand Inland Revenue Department, Tax Technical "Income Tax – Timing of Disposal and Derivation of Income from Trading Stock" BR PUB 14/08 (30 September 2014) available at <www.taxtechnical.ird.govt.nz/>.
32    "Until 19 September 1985 Australia had no capital gains tax. There were, however, two important provisions of the ITAA 1936 that equated capital gains tax with income – s 25A and s 26AAA, which treated profits on the sale of property purchased and sold within 12 months as assessable income. Despite those two sections and some others throughout ITAA 1936 that assessed amounts that would not otherwise be income, as a basic principle, prior to 19 September 1985, capital amounts were not taxed." Robert Deutsch et al, *Australian Tax Handbook 2000* (ATP, 2000) 242.
33    *McClelland v Federal Commissioner of Taxation* [1970] UKPCHCA 1; (1970) 120 CLR 487.

the sale of assets (capital gains) and revenue received from trading according to ordinary concepts — the sale of trading stock.

## 3.2 The Review of Published Literature

Expenditure falls into three broad categories: payments for the purchase of revenue assets for sale — trading stock; payments to provide for the operation of the enterprise on a day-to-day basis; and payments for long-term or capital assets that are used to produce goods or services for sale.

Prior to examining published literature to determine a definition of assets, capital and revenue, this book considers the following dictionary definitions. The definitions may not be legally binding in providing legal distinctions between the accounting concepts considered in this study, but they do form a useful basis for considering such distinctions.

The official dictionary for the *Australian Guide to Legal Citation*,[34] the *Macquarie Dictionary*, defines assets as *"commerce* resources of a person or business consisting of such items as real property, machinery, inventories, notes, securities, cash etc".[35] Capital is defined as "the wealth, whether in money or property, owned or used in business by an individual, firm, etc; an accumulated stock of such wealth; [and] any form of wealth used, or capable of being used in the production of more wealth".[36] It defines revenue as "the collective items or amounts of income of a person, a state, etc. [or] return or yield from any kind of property".[37]

The *Oxford Dictionary* defines assets as "any property or effects available to meet the debts of a testator, debtor or company whether sufficient or not".[38] It defines capital as "the stock with which a company or person enters into business; the total sum of

---

34    Melbourne University Law Review *Australian Guide to Legal Citation* (4th ed, 2018).
35    Colin Yallop and others (eds) *Macquarie Concise Dictionary* (4th ed, 2006) 62 'assets' (def 1).
36    Ibid 179 'capital' (def 3).
37    Ibid 1042 'revenue' (def 2).
38    Angus Stevenson (ed), *Shorter Oxford English Dictionary: On Historical Principles* (6th ed, 2007) 'asset' (def 2).

shareholders' contributions in a joint-stock company; accumulated wealth, *esp*, as used in further production".[39] Revenue is defined as "income *spec* from property, possessions, or investment, esp, of an extensive kind".[40]

Significant to this study is the Yorston, Smyth and Brown definition of stock-in-trade as:

the aggregate of those items of tangible property which are:

1. held for sale in the ordinary course of business, or
2. in the process of production for such sale, or
3. to be currently consumed in the production of goods or services to be available for sale.[41]

It is inferred that the distinction between fixed and current assets is the time taken to convert the asset to cash. In particular, for taxation purposes, that definition of duration is significant for the distinction between an asset and a revenue expense. A fixed asset may take some time and cost to convert to cash and have a significant impact on the operations of an enterprise. In contrast, a current asset is either cash or is readily converted to cash within a short time. In the main, the sale of current assets is part of the normal operations of an enterprise, while the sale of a fixed asset is not.

However, the 1975 Asprey Report noted that all livestock are considered as trading stock. It suggested that changes in the closing value of livestock would have an impact on income for taxation purposes.[42] The Asprey Report states:

All livestock in a business of primary production are treated by the Act as trading stock even though some animals are not acquired for the purpose of sale. [43]

---

39    Ibid 342 'capital' (def B2).
40    Ibid 2563 'revenue' (def 2).
41    Keith Yorston, Eugene Bryan Smyth and Samuel Raymond Brown, *Advanced Accounting* (Law Book, 1978) 12. This definition is based on the definition of 'Inventory' as contained in Chapter 4, *Accounting Research Bulletin*, No 43, 1953 of the American Institute of Accountants.
42    Ibid, 105–106.
43    Taxation Review Committee, *Full Report* (Parliamentary Paper No 136, January 1975) (Asprey Report) 99.

However, it further considered that some livestock, such as stud stock, could form part of the assets of a business along with the plant. It states:

> Although animals not acquired for the purpose of sale (for example, stud stock) could be regarded as more akin to plant than trading stock, there is no provision in the Act for writing off annual amounts of depreciation from their cost.[44]

and

> For this purpose, the provision of capital and property to a partnership would not only include funds and assets overtly contributed as partnership capital. It would also extend to property, including loan moneys made available for use in the partnership business without recompense or on favourable terms, and any other benefit given or granted to the partnership by one or more partners but not by all partners according to their shares, such as land, livestock, plant, goodwill, etc. owned by one partner but used by the partnership without realistic recompense. [45]

Therefore, it is argued that the Asprey Report is inconclusive in its findings as to the classification of livestock as current assets (revenue items) or capital assets (capital items).

From the Asprey Report, it appears that if stud stock were to be depreciated, then they may well be considered as plant. The report also points to the influence of accounting treatment for distributing the capital cost over several accounting periods in helping to determine if livestock kept for stud purposes should be revenue or capital items.

Bazley and others support their definition of assets by quoting the Statement of Accounting Concepts (SAC 4):[46] "Assets are future economic benefits controlled by the entity as a result of past transactions or other past events."[47]

---

44   Ibid 283.
45   Ibid 150.
46   The Public Sector Accounting Standards Board of the Australian Accounting Research Foundation and the Australian Accounting Standards Board "Statement of Accounting Concepts SAC 4 (3/95) Definition and Recognition of the Elements of Financial Statements" (1995) available at <www.aasb.gov.au>.
47   Michael Bazley et al, *Contemporary Accounting: A Conceptual Approach* (3rd ed, Nelson Australia, 1999) 49; see also Garry Carnegie et al, *Financial Accounting: Financial and Organisational Decision Making* (McGraw-Hill, 1999) 66.

Revenue is defined by Bazley and others as:

> inflows or other enhancements, or savings in outflows, of future economic benefits in the form of increases in assets or reductions in liabilities of the entity, other than those relating to contributions by owners, that result in an increase in equity during the reporting period (SAC 4, para 111). [48]

The distinction between assets and revenue as defined by Bazley and others is that assets are a means of creating economic benefits, and revenue is the economic benefit created by the asset. *The Accounting Handbook 2001* also prescribes the definitions set out in SAC 4 for use by members of CPA Australia and the Institute of Chartered Accountants in Australia.[49]

The historical perspective of the recognition of property, plant and equipment changed in Australia with the introduction of the Australian Accounting Standard AASB 116 in 2005.[50] The standard has been amended since that time and its application as of January 2020 is as follows:

> This compiled Standard applies to annual periods beginning on or after 1 January 2019 but before 1 January 2021. Earlier application is permitted for annual periods beginning on or after 1 January 2014 but before 1 January 2019. It incorporates relevant amendments made up to and including 9 December 2016. [51]

Broader discussion of AASB 116 is beyond the scope of this research, but it is noted that AASB 116 was enacted in compliance with Australia's international obligations imposed in accordance with the International Accounting Standard (IAS) 16 "Presentation of Financial Statements", as issued and amended by the International Accounting Standards Board (IASB).

Of relevance is the objective of AASB 116, which is

---

48    Ibid 51.
49    Colin Parker (ed) *Accounting Handbook 2001: Volume 1 of the Accounting and Auditing Handbook 2001* (Prentice Hall, 2001) 35; see also Michele A Sims and Robert Charles Clift *Australian Corporate Accounting: The Formulation, Expansion and Dissolution of Companies* (McGraw-Hill, 2001) 74, 173; Craig Deegan *Financial Accounting Theory* (McGraw-Hill, 2001) 134.
50    Australian Accounting Standards Board *Accounting Standards AASB 116* (2019) <www.aasb.gov.au/>.
51    Ibid.

to prescribe the accounting treatment for property, plant and equipment so that users of the financial statements can discern information about an entity's investment in its property, plant and equipment and the changes in such investment. The principal issues in accounting for property, plant and equipment are the recognition of the assets, the determination of their carrying amounts and the depreciation charges and impairment losses to be recognised in relation to them. [52]

It states:

> Property, plant and equipment are tangible items that:
> (a)       are held for use in the production or supply of goods or services, for rental to others, or for administrative purposes; and
> (b)       are expected to be used during more than one period. [53]

AASB 116 defines plant and equipment as tangible items for use for more than one [accounting] period (year). It is suggested that retaining an animal for production of saleable assets for a number of years gives substance to the argument that animals retained for production purposes are plant and therefore a capital asset, rather than stock held for trading purposes.

AASB 116 appears to settle the argument from an accounting perspective. However, it does not apply to:

> (b)       biological assets related to agricultural activity other than bearer plants (see AASB 141 "Agriculture"). [54]

Therefore, this part examines the accounting compliance requirements set out in Accounting Standard AASB 141 "Agriculture".[55] It is noted that AASB 141 was enacted in compliance with Australia's international obligations imposed in accordance with International Accounting Standard (IAS) 14 "Agriculture".

The examination seeks to establish the impact of AASB 141 on the classification of biological assets as current (revenue) or non-current (capital) assets. Further, it seeks to clarify whether AASB 116 is to be totally ignored when accounting for biological assets.

---

52   Ibid.
53   Ibid [7].
54   Ibid [3(b)].
55   Australian Accounting Standards Board *Accounting Standards AASB 141* (2019) available at <www.aasb.gov.au/>.

As with the examination of AASB 116, this examination is restricted to the elements that are the focus of this book and is not intended to be an in-depth examination of the accounting standard.

Significantly, AASB 141 defines a *biological asset* as a living animal or plant.[56] Dairy cattle for the production of milk, the focus of the *Wade Case*, are provided as an example of biological assets.[57] Hence, AASB 141 applies to the accounting treatment of the cattle held for breeding purposes.

AASB 141 gives examples to illustrate the distinction between 'consumable biological assets' as being agricultural assets which

> are those that are to be harvested as agricultural produce or sold as biological assets. Examples of consumable biological assets are livestock intended for the production of meat, livestock held for sale, fish in farms, crops such as maize and wheat, produce on a bearer plant and trees being grown for lumber.

and

> 'bearer biological assets' as agricultural assets which:[58]
> are those other than consumable biological assets; for example, livestock from which milk is produced and fruit trees from which fruit is harvested. Bearer biological assets are not agricultural produce but, rather, are held to bear produce. [59]

It is argued that animals held for breeding livestock for sale are bearer biological assets (capital) and not consumable biological assets (revenue), as are the dairy cattle described in AASB 141. Of relevance to this book is that the standard specifically refers to 'non-current' biological assets and how they are to be treated once they meet the criteria to be classified as being held for sale and therefore become held as current assets.[60]

AASB 141 details how biological assets are to be valued and reported for financial accounting disclosure purposes. Chiefly, it acknowledges the vagaries of market values of biological assets as

---

56  Ibid [5].
57  Ibid [4].
58  Ibid.
59  Ibid [44].
60  Ibid [30].

a consequence of a range of natural and economic influences on their value from time to time.

It appears the key philosophy of AASB 141 is that historical cost valuations, generally used in accounting conventions, and in particular AASB 116, are inappropriate for a true and accurate disclosure of value when accounting for biological assets. It specifically acknowledges variations in value due to:

> biological transformation results in the following types of outcomes:
> (a)    asset changes through (i) growth (an increase in quantity or improvement in quality of an animal or plant), (ii) degeneration (a decrease in the quantity or deterioration in quality of an animal or plant), or (iii) procreation (creation of additional living animals or plants); or
> (b)    production of agricultural produce such as latex, tea leaf, wool, and milk. [61]

Further, it does not function as an alternative accounting standard to AASB 116 but rather as a complement to it and other standards:

> In determining cost, accumulated depreciation and accumulated impairment losses, an entity considers AASB 102, AASB 116 and AASB 136 Impairment of Assets. [62]

It is therefore appropriate that the Australian Accounting Standards are a valid support for the argument of this book that livestock held for breeding purposes for at least more than one accounting period are capital assets and not stock in trade, that is, revenue items.

Fischer and Marsh[63] examined the generally accepted accounting principles (GAAP) existing in the United States at that time to explore the impact of the adoption of the international accounting guidance for agricultural activities. They found that "there [were] systematic differences between the US generally accepted

---

61    Ibid [7].
62    Ibid [33].
63    Mary Fischer and Treba Marsh "Biological Assets: Financial Recognition and Reporting Using US and International Accounting Guidance" (2013) 13(2) *Journal of Accounting and Finance* 57.

accounting principles and International accounting and reporting for agricultural assets and products".[64]

They also found:

> that international and US agricultural accounting recognition and reporting guidance results in dissimilar reporting due to guidance interpretation. IAS 41 is an effort to improve comparability of agricultural companies' financial statement. However, valuation variances and definition differences including the requirement to change the agricultural asset recognition method from historical cost to fair value continue to be the basis of major reporting differences. [65]

They point to the complexities of market vagaries regarding developing animals. They consider the example of the growth of a newborn animal. They state:

> the assigned value using LCM [lower of cost or market] value to a newborn would be zero. For the first 3 to 10 months of an infant's life cycle, the newborn only requires the mother's milk and the only cost allocated to the newborn would only be the boarding. This presents a valuation issue as GAAP Codification 905 guidance recognizes 3-month-old calves at zero on the balance sheet when in the Western US cattle producing area 3 to 6-month-old calves have a fair market value of $200 to $300 or higher. [66]

They considered the dilemma of breeding and production animals reaching maturity and the base value for depreciation. Their example suggests that the cost of a two-year-old heifer could reasonably be established, but what if the livestock market at the point of annual valuation is less than that cost and the market range is between US$600 and US$1,300?[67]

An issue that could also be considered is the point in time at which the animal is classified as a breeding or production animal and no longer trading stock. Cattle under the mature age of 15 months could not be considered breeding stock, but what if the cattle beast is 24 months of age?

By determining that an animal that is held for more than one accounting period (year) becomes a breeding or production animal

---

64    Ibid 68.
65    Ibid.
66    Ibid 59.
67    Ibid.

or by defining ALL livestock as trading stock, the dilemma of annual valuations and classification of breeding or production stock and stock for resale is avoided. However, it does not comply with the accounting compliance provisions of AASB 141. The adoption of AASB 141 creates a tax effect accounting reconciliation matter for tax preparers.

A further consideration of this book is that a finding that compensation paid to Wade in 1951 was of a capital nature may have exempted those monies from taxation entirely. However, capital gains tax was introduced in 1985, and div 108 of the ITAA 1997 now applies to the imposition of capital gains tax on capital gains and losses from the acquisition and disposal of capital assets.

It is noted that the provisions of s 118-20 act to prevent the imposition of both income tax and capital gains tax on the same transaction. The levy of tax on gains or losses from the sale of livestock held for breeding purposes is not disputed but rather the type of tax levied — income tax or capital gains tax.

This review looked at the interpretation of the Asprey Report which considered ALL livestock as trading stock but then stated that some livestock, such as stud stock, could form part of the assets of a business along with plant.

It also considered that a consistent criterion for defining current and non-current assets is the ownership over several accounting periods (years). That stud stock are held for many seasons (years) lends weight to the argument that stud stock are more likely to be non-current assets than stock in trade held for the singular purpose of resale for a profit.

The following section details the design of the research paradigm conducted to substantiate its findings and conclusions.

## 3.3  Research Design and Conduct

A combination of quantitative and qualitative research approaches was adopted to support the findings of this book. The mixed methods or multi-method research approach[68] was adopted to support the narrative.

Yin suggests that whilst quantitative surveys are a commonly used method for collecting and analysing empirical evidence, there is a need to engage in qualitative case studies to address the questions of 'how' and 'why'.[69] He indicates that the case study strategy has distinct advantages, particularly where the research is focussed on the question of *why*.[70]

Other researchers also support the use of a mixed methods approach. In assessing the validity of qualitative interviews, Merriam[71] argues that whilst quantitative research exposes the facts and clearly illustrates *what* is happening, it cannot discover the 'reality' itself.[72] Further, John Sydenstricker-Neto points out weaknesses in the singular use of statistical analysis, or quantitative research, and suggests that: "[a]dding qualitative flesh to the quantitative bones is a good strategy to overcoming some of these problems".[73]

The book seeks not only to assess what is understood by tax preparers to be the appropriate classification of animals in accounting terms but also why they have established that understanding.

For the purposes of consistency, both the quantitative survey and qualitative study consider the same hypothetical scenario which was presented to both survey participants and case study interviewees. Although it is based on a hypothetical scenario, this

---

68    Mathew B Miles and A Michael Huberman *Qualitative Data Analysis* (2nd ed, Sage, 1994) 2; Juliet Corbin and Anselm Strauss *Basics of Qualitative Research* (3rd ed, Sage, 2008) 25; Jane Elliott *Using Narrative in Social Research: Qualitative and Quantitative Approaches* (Sage, 2005) 157–159; Michael Crotty *The Foundations of Social Research: Meaning and Perspective in the Research Process* (Sage, 2003) 15; John Wade Creswell *Research Design; Qualitative, Quantitative and Mixed Methods Approaches* (2nd ed, Sage, 2003) 17; Margaret McKerchar *Design and Conduct of Research in Tax, Law and Accounting* (Thomson Reuters, 2010).

69    Robert K Yin *Case Study Research: Design and Methods* (3rd ed, Sage, 2003) 6.

70    Ibid. Yin categorises research questions as 'who', 'what', 'where', 'how' and 'why'.

71    Sharan B Merriam *Qualitative Research and Case Study Applications in Education* (2nd ed, Jossey-Bass, 1998).

72    Ibid 202.

73    John Sydenstricker-Neto "Research Design and Mixed-Method Approach: A Hands-on Experience" (1997) <www.socialresearchmethods.net/>.

case study could also be applied to almost any rural property or farm carrying livestock for commercial purposes in Australia. The study used a Likert scale from one to five, ranging from 'all animals are breeding stock (capital)' to 'all animals are trading stock (revenue)', or combinations of both in between to answer the research question: "On the sale of a rural business (farm or pastoral lease) involving livestock, are all animals (cattle, sheep, goats and the like) considered as trading stock and therefore revenue items? Alternatively, are some, or all, animals breeding stock and therefore subject to capital gains tax provisions and exemptions?"

The quantitative survey conducted as grounding for this research gives an indicator of *what* is understood as the 'correct' interpretation of the classification of livestock. It also indicated the dominant interpretation by the broader population of tax preparers.

This research then looked at the underlying question of *why* they established that understanding. A number of interviews were conducted with persons engaged in the sale of Outback pastoral leases in Western Australia. They were interviewed to assess what they believe to be an appropriate approach to classifying animals for accounting and taxation purposes. They were asked their opinions as to whether animals could be considered as stock for breeding, or stud, and therefore capital items, or as livestock for sale and therefore revenue items.

The scope of interviewees consisted of:

- a rural-based accountant/tax preparer from northern Victoria;
- an urban-based accountant/tax preparer from the city of Perth in Western Australia;
- a purchaser of a pastoral property in the Northwest of Western Australia;
- the executor of a vendor of a pastoral property in the Northwest of Western Australia;
- a licensed real estate and business agent engaged in the sale of rural and pastoral properties in Western Australia; and

- a person engaged in the pastoral industry in the Northwest of Western Australia.

It was considered that those interviewees covered a broad scope of experience and opinions from a range of relevant perspectives. They were interviewed to provide insights into how those engaged in the pastoral industry view the distinction between livestock raised for sale as trading stock and those animals kept for breeding or stud stock to maintain their production herds.

To support the qualitative study, an ATO ruling was sought on the hypothetical case study, and a taxpayer also provided the contract of sale and income tax return for the purpose of analysis of the sale of a property in April 2017.

Further, in its advice, the ATO stated that it relied on the findings in the *Wade Case* to form the opinion that "[t]he Commissioner considers that the definition of livestock in section 995-1 of the Income Tax Assessment Act 1997 includes all animals in a primary production business".[74] Hence, the findings in the *Wade Case* are also examined to support or refute that opinion and to increase confidence in the conclusions of this part.

The following chapter compares the findings of the quantitative and qualitative research to conclude whether the prevailing interpretation of the ATO and Australian tax preparers is appropriate. It also quantifies the applicable taxation burden of the alternative classifications — are the animals transferred on the sale of a rural property 'mother' (capital) or 'meat' (revenue), or a combination of both?

---

74  Lendon (n 18).

# Chapter Four
# The Research Outcomes and Analysis

## 4.1 Case Study Analysis — Tax Practitioner Survey

While there are 42,501 individual tax practitioners registered as tax agents as of October 2019,[75] the Tax Practitioners Board was unable to identify precisely how many agents are active or the number of practices that exist. It further advised that "[m]any agents can work for other entities and also have a practice themselves".[76] Therefore, the total population of tax agencies in public practice is unknown.

The Institute of Public Accountants (IPA) advised that it had 3,060 active public practitioners in Australia.[77] While the IPA is a significant professional accounting body in Australia, its membership is somewhat less than that of the Chartered Accountants Australia and New Zealand. Nonetheless, the population of 3,000 active practitioners out of a total membership of about 35,000 indicates that the number of active tax practitioners in Australia may be less than 10,000.

However, as this research focuses on rural properties, and given that the volume of sales of pastoral leases in Western Australia was only 361 over 38 years, compared to an estimated 2.6 million land transfers, the population of tax preparers who have encountered the sale of pastoral leases in Australia is likely to be comparatively few.

Further, the survey focussed on rural practitioners because it was assumed that they would be more likely to experience pastoral land sales than urban practitioners. As the total population of tax practitioners who have compiled income tax returns for taxpayers who have transferred pastoral leases cannot be accurately

---

75  Tax Practitioners' Board, "Search the Register" (2019) available at <www.tpb.go v.au>.

76  Email from Client Support Team, Tax Practitioners' Board, to Alexander Fullarton, 28 November 2019.

77  Email from Laura Baynes, Institute of Public Accountants to Alexander Fullarton, 21 October 2019.

determined, assumptions have been made using the above comparatives.

If the total population of individual tax practitioners is somewhat less than 42,501 and the ratio of pastoral sales to total land transfers is 0.0139 per cent (based on the Western Australia statistics), then only six tax preparers would be expected to have experience with the conduct of pastoral land sales in Western Australia. Only 12 practising CPA public practitioners could be found beyond the Adelaide metropolitan area in South Australia. However, two urban-based practices were found that had rural clients.

Intuitively, the total population of rural-based tax preparers is likely to be extremely small compared to the total population of registered tax practitioners. Therefore, a quantitative survey of 96 public tax practitioners of the Institute of Public Accountants was conducted.

Three attempts were made to engage those accounting practices by electronic mail, and direct contact by staff of the Institute was conducted over a period of 12 months. At the conclusion of the survey, 14 responses were received. A further telephone survey of 14 South Australian CPAs was conducted, from which five responses were obtained.

Table 1 shows the number of responses in each category from 1 'all animals are breeding stock (capital)' to 5 'all animals are trading stock (revenue)' and the ratios in between (25/75; 50/50; and 25/75 of breeding to trade stock).

| Category | 1 | 2 | 3 | 4 | 5 | total | population |
|---|---|---|---|---|---|---|---|
| Aust IPA responses | 0 | 1 | 3 | 4 | 6 | 14 | 96 |
| SA CPA reponses | 1 | 0 | 1 | 0 | 3 | 5 | 14 |
| sub-total | 1 | 1 | 4 | 4 | 9 | 19 | 110 |
| percentage | 5,26 | 5,26 | 21,05 | 21,05 | 47,37 | 100 | |

Table 1: Table of Survey Responses: Mother or Meat Survey of Tax Preparers.[78]

By considering the Null Hypothesis 'Not ALL Australian tax preparers agree with the ATO view that ALL animals in a primary

---

[78]    The estimate of the total population of rural tax preparers was established from the postcodes declared to be the area of operations of IPA and CPA members published on the Institute websites.

production business are livestock for trading purposes', from the raw data, the number of those who do consider ALL animals livestock (category 5) is compared to those who do not (categories 1–4). A chi-square test of 0.0219873 is obtained using the Excel spreadsheet program. That indicates the survey is statistically significant.

The survey found that only one of the respondents considered all of the animals in the proposed hypothetical scenario as capital, despite only some of those animals being held for breeding purposes and others, such as calves, being of no commercial value. Yet, less than half of the respondents determined that they were ALL trade stock, with 52.6 per cent favouring the concept that at least some of the animals should be classified as breeding stock to varying degrees.

The scale 1 respondent detailed a reasonably complex accounting and registration system that should be maintained to ensure the numbers and values of breeding stock were kept segregated from the trading stock. She suggested that the animals considered to be of no commercial value at the point of transfer be recorded in the Livestock Trading Account by number at no monetary value. At the point of sale of those animals sometime in the future when they had reached trade weight and therefore were of commercial value, then the profit would be accurately disclosed in the Livestock Trading Account.

A comment from one of the respondents who scored 3 on the scale (either breeding stock or trading stock) was:

> Stock that is purchased for resale is trading stock and would be treated as such if the farm or lease was sold. Stock that is not purchased for resale (breeding) should be treated as an active business asset and depreciated the same as any other asset. There are current rulings that deal with race horses and other livestock. If the breeding stock is sold in the process of the farm sale, the disposal can only be on income account. The same condition applies if you were to sell general plant and equipment; this will never be on capital account. The accounting profit being the difference between the written down value of the asset and the consideration received.

It appears the respondent is accounting for a profit or loss on the sale of breeding stock as an extraordinary profit or loss in the revenue statement, and it is income according to ordinary concepts, rather than a capital loss or gain for CGT purposes. Another scale 3 respondent commented:

> The tax treatment would greatly depend on numbers. We would consider writing off lame animals, those kept for breeding, treat as breeding stock and those left treat as stock not kept for breeding.

A scale 4 respondent commented:

> 60 per cent IT and 40 per cent CGT provisions would seem fair for properties in remote Australia (shrublands). An actual split/classification for other regions.

Interestingly, the respondent added:

> From my experience, most 'farmers' don't pay very much tax at all. The only time they really contribute to the revenue of Australia is when they finally sell up and the livestock is treated as trading stock (IT provisions). Maybe treating 'livestock' as an active asset but no discount would be a fair compromise.

This respondent appears to have a value judgment that farmers receive favouritism from the taxation system and do not pay their 'fair share' of tax. The discussion of tax minimisation schemes is beyond the scope of this research. For an in-depth analysis of taxpayer attitudes toward tax minimisation, Fullarton investigated taxpayer engagement in the mass-marketed tax avoidance schemes of the 1990s.[79]

A scale 5 respondent adopted a practical philosophy:

> I can see possibilities though think it would have to stay as trading stock for reasons:

1. Too hard to police separation of trading stock from breeding stock.
2. Breeding stock losses from deaths or any other reason would logically be a capital loss and in most (primary producer) cases would be a nuisance as they generally have a low incidence of use for capital losses (that can only offset against cap gains).

---

79    Alexander Robert Fullarton *Heat, Dust and Taxes: A Story of Tax Schemes in Australia's Outback* (Ibidem Verlag, 2014).

Another scale 5 respondent also reflected the practical nature of animal classification. He considered the matter simply:

> It should be 3 but usually it is too late for the accountant to have any input [in the allocation of funds which make up the total price the sale of the property.

The final scale 5 respondent who commented acknowledged there could be CGT provisions if breeding stock were separated, but they are not. Therefore, considering all animals as trading stock provides for the "equitable cost base for the purchaser's livestock profit and loss business [account]".

Despite inaccuracies that may arise from a survey population of just 19 respondents, the survey indicates that tax preparers are much divided in their perspectives as to the classification of livestock. Nearly all, including those who hold the opinion that ALL livestock are trading stock, acknowledged that breeding stock should be considered separately as active assets, even if the accounts were not kept in that fashion.

It is suggested that although many of the animals are not considered separately as breeding stock and therefore subject to CGT and related concessions, that decision is influenced by other factors.

Some of those other factors include the attitude of one respondent that considering ALL livestock as trading stock would be a method by which "farmers finally pay their 'fair share' of tax". That was justified from a social justice point of view rather than lawful or economic equity, even if it arose from inaccurate accounting treatment on the sale of their properties.

A view held by a respondent implied that farmers 'fiddled the system' and did not pay their fair share of tax throughout their farming life, so it is fair that they overpay their tax in the end. Further discussion as to the equity or fairness of tax liability of farmers arising from the classification of livestock as trading stock is beyond the scope of this research.

To add qualitative 'meat' to the quantitative 'bones'[80] of the survey, the book now examines the opinions of other stakeholders

---

80   Sydenstricker-Neto (n 73).

in the sale of pastoral properties, including two tax preparers, to boost reader confidence in the findings of this research.

## 4.2 Case Study Analysis — Stakeholder Interviews

Seven persons contributed to the stakeholder interviews, including a vendor, their respective agents and a purchaser of a pastoral property in Western Australia.

The study also included long-term pastoralists. They were descendants of three generations of a family engaged in the pastoral industry and have no intention of selling in the foreseeable future, if at all, but rather passing the ownership on to the following family generations. Their opinion was sought as independent support for how transactions relating to herds were managed and classified on modern pastoral properties, at least in Western Australia.

The analysis will follow the pattern of involvement of stakeholders in relation to owning and operating a pastoral lease through the process of selling the property to the new owner.

The stakeholders interviewed by occupation were:

- two pastoralists from the Gascoyne region of Western Australia;
- a vendor of a pastoral property;
- a pastoral lease broker;
- a purchaser of a pastoral property;
- a rural public accountant/tax preparer from northern Victoria; and
- an urban public accountant/tax preparer from Perth in Western Australia.

The study found that all of the interviewees stated that they were familiar with the sale of pastoral properties. However, the number of transactions that they had been involved in was very limited. The exception to that situation was the professional licensed real estate agent and pastoral lease broker who had specialised in the sale of pastoral leases in Western Australia for decades. He had been involved in dozens of sales over the years. This reflects the limited number of pastoral property sales disclosed by the Landgate statistics discussed previously.

**Pastoralist one** was a person who had inherited his property. He had been directly involved in the pastoral industry for about 20 years and indirectly involved through his family for his entire life.

He was familiar with the hypothetical case put to him and had heard of similar transactions, but he had never been involved in the sale of a property other than transfers within the family. In addition, he was not entirely familiar with Australian capital gains tax provisions and exemptions.

He remarked that he would not purchase the station described in the hypothetical case. He said he did not trust the figures presented and said:

> I wouldn't buy the station. Not unless I was present at that muster, and therefore present every day after until the end of the six weeks until the transfer occurred, that sale transaction would not be current as it has been highlighted recently, numbers differentiate between what is so-called 'on the books' and what is on the property. [81]

His concern as to numbers of cattle transferred was focused on the quid pro quo of the transaction rather than the categorisation of breeding stock and livestock for trade and is beyond the scope of this research, but he makes a valid point. The numbers and value of animals are extremely fluid. That is a central focus of AASB 141, discussed earlier.

As to stock on hand and the allocation of proceeds from the sale of the property, he made this observation:

> Right, cows, you would count cows and you don't count calves. You just count cows and anything over weaners. Your cow/calf units are usually classed as, are just put in as cows. You just count them as whatever they are like at the going price at a recent sale. Roughly would be an indicator but usually most stations are sold on a head number.
>
> You don't actually put a value on the homestead, furniture and such for the price of the sale. That comes later when you divvy it up. But usually, cattle stations are sold as a 20,000-unit cattle place which would go for about two

---

81    Interview with Participant P 6 (Telephone Interview with Alexander Robert Fullarton, Curtin Law School, 30 June 2019).

times the current value at the stage of a cow which is probably near enough to about $2,000 a head. [82]

He elaborated on the allocation of funds for the sale of the property and suggested the following method of categorisation:

> Well, you do then design a value to which would bring that capital of expenditure on the animals back from $2,000 a head, which is what you would be buying the station at and then you would divvy[83] it off to the market value for the graders or market value for the infrastructure but, really, it is sort of designed; the pastoral lease is actually designed as how many cattle are on there, and that is why you pay a higher price per cow.[84]

In the event the property was unstocked, he considered the concept of 'potential value'. He said "potential value is what you would be looking at then. So, it would have a value of the plant, the value of the lease and the value of the vegetation of what you are going to graze".[85]

He saw no distinction between stud or breeding stock and livestock bred for sale. He suggested that all animals were the same—ultimately, they were all going to be sold. He said

> Herd bulls go on the truck just as easy as normal bulls. They could be broken down.[86] Once they go on the truck, their value really diminishes but their value diminishes once you buy them and put them on a pastoral lease. [87]

He elaborated.

> Well, you go and buy a $6,000 bull, whose kilo value is probably let's say $2 a kilo, and he's weighing in at eight hundred kilos which is commercial down at ahh, put him across the Muchea floor,[88] the saleyard floor would be a value of sixteen hundred dollars; as soon as you get into the pastoral country, anything could happen to him. It's just about a direct write-off, really, once they get to the pastoral region. They can break a dick, get a seed in there or whatever and become useless. [89]

---

82    Ibid.
83    An Australian colloquialism for 'divide' or share out.
84    Ibid.
85    Participant P 6 (n 81).
86    Become sterile.
87    Ibid.
88    Livestock saleyards near Perth in Western Australia.
89    Participant P 6 (n 81).

This participant's view strongly supports the view held in the *Wade Case* and that of the ATO.

**The vendor** had recently conducted and settled a sale for and on behalf of the estate of a deceased person and was very familiar with the process. She had also been a settlement agent in Western Australia for many decades and was very familiar with the process of transfers of property. She had been involved in the lodgement of the final income tax return in relation to the estate and had success-fully appealed the original assessment, which had been prepared and lodged by an accountant.

The original income tax return and assessment considered that ALL livestock were trading stock in accordance with the general ATO opinion supported by the *Wade Case*.[90] She appealed on the basis that ALL of the trade livestock had been mustered and re-moved from the property in a separate transaction. ALL of the re-maining animals were either those of no commercial value or a breeding stock for the continued operations of the property.

She stated

> I feel that they should have treated as part of the infrastructure necessary to run the station. I think it is fair and reasonable that the cattle that were sold at muster [to be treated as trading stock]. That a complete muster was done so those ones were trade cattle. Yes, they were part of the income for that financial year but the cattle which remained.
>
> Bearing in mind that for a pastoral lease, it is one of the — it is essential, it is part of the infrastructure that you have to keep a base amount of cattle there; otherwise, it is not a workable concern. You have to do this to comply with the pastoral lease and in addition, those breeding stock are absolutely nec-essary to maintain the running of the station, and if you don't maintain the running of the station, I mean, for example, if you sold every single animal, then you would not be complying with the terms of your pastoral lease an-yway. So, I think they are integral to the running of the station and the lease.[91]

She supported her argument by noting that a requirement of a pas-toral lease in Western Australia is that a minimum operational stock level must be maintained. The stock mustered and sold

---

90   Lendon (n 18).
91   Interview with Participant P 3 (Telephone Interview with Alexander Robert Fullarton, Curtin Law School, 13 March 2019).

immediately prior to the sale had been treated as trading stock in the livestock trading account. Those of no commercial value were taken up by the purchaser at that value, and any profit from the sale of that stock would be reflected in the purchaser's livestock trading account. That accounting perspective appears to be in compliance with AASB 141 discussed previously.

The amendment was accepted on review, and the capital gains tax concessions accompanying the CGT levied on the sale of the breeding stock was accepted by the ATO. It is noted that the distinction between livestock for trading purposes and animals kept for production had been clearly and distinctly classified with supporting statistics, registrations and other supporting documentation.

This participant had made the distinction between stud or breeding stock and livestock for trade and had argued her case accordingly, with supporting documentary evidence.

**The pastoral lease broker** was a Western Australian business broker with decades of experience focussing on the sale of pastoral leases. He was aware of the distinction between livestock held as trading stock according to ordinary concepts and livestock retained by farmers for the purpose of breeding.

However, he said that he did not make the distinction when dealing with the sale of pastoral leases and farming properties and was also negatively critical of the United States concept of a timing criterion to distinguish breeding stock from livestock.[92]

Anecdotally, it is believed that in the United States, animals are classified according to their age: all younger animals (less than 12 months old) are considered livestock for trading, and those older than 24 months are deliberately kept for breeding.

This participant said "That is a bloody stupid idea. What happens in the case where you have a three-year-old steer? Surely you can't consider a steer as breeding stock, no matter how old it is." [93] In response to the question, "Why are you holding a steer for more

---

92　Fischer and Marsh (n 63) 59. Fischer and Marsh did not consider neutered or sterilised animals.

93　Interview with Participant P 2 (Telephone Interview with Alexander Robert Fullarton, Curtin Law School, 4 July 2017).

than two years?" He replied, "It simply hasn't hit trade weight yet. But it will be sold as soon as it is."[94]

It is suggested that his opinions may be due to a misunderstanding of IAS 41, or an interpretation of how the United States livestock industry operates. Examination of that concept is beyond the scope of this research, but the timing structure for continual valuation, under the provisions of IAS 41 and AASB 141, might give some substance to that understanding.

In the Australian experience, where much livestock is held on unimproved rangelands, it may take many years for beasts to reach a commercially viable trading weight. Therefore, the United States timing criterion may not be a reliable indicator of breeding/trading stock classification diversity.

When questioned as to how he had come to understand and actively discriminate between animals used as breeding stock and trading stock, he said he was also an experienced farmer and therefore well acquainted with the minutiae of classification of farm animals.

He stated that he not only listed livestock according to breeding and trading stock on negotiated contracts of sale, but he also appended a schedule of inventory which classified livestock according to type, such as cows with calves, heifers, weaned calves, steers, bulls and the like.

However, he said the sale price was normally agreed upon by negotiating a gross sale price.

> What we tend to do is just come up with a number that is across the board — an average across the board and put a price to it. Not necessarily per head but put a value to all the stock in one lump. That's how we normally do it. You know our values are arrived at by what sort of breeding stock the properties can run, and you know what's on the property at the time, and usually it's a guestimate because we can only go on current mustering figures. You know mustering figures which may be six months old. And then sometimes you estimate some calves. You estimate what may or may not be there. . .. That can be done. I'm not suggesting it can't be done, but as a general rule, you would just be going with a lump sum for the livestock.[95]

---

94   Ibid.
95   Ibid.

He advised that he had developed the practice of livestock classification and the appendix of the inventory through many years of experience. That experience was not only as a farmer but also industry experience in conducting rural property sales.

He pointed out that he had not adopted the practice from attending industry forums or training from real estate industry bodies to gain that method of sales practice, although the concept of an itemised list of stock or 'stocktake' is not uncommon. As far as he was concerned, his method of dealing with livestock was simply a matter of professional due diligence and the correct approach to documenting the sale of rural properties.

It is rather common practice for the sale of businesses in Australia to conduct a stocktake at the point of transfer of ownership of the business.[96] Most businesses are transferred subject to an itemised list and valuation of stock at the point of transfer. It is therefore unusual to encounter a different practice for the transfer of stock in the case under review.

This participant also made the distinction between stud or breeding stock and livestock for trade. He also stated that the distinction should be supported with sound documentary evidence but considered that record keeping and account keeping were beyond his role as a broker.

> I am just aware that there is a transaction levy when stock are transferred and whether they are breeding stock or whether they are stud stock or whatever they are. I am not aware of a difference. There may well be a difference and probably that might be sorted out by the accountants, but we don't get involved with that.[97]

He made several other comments to illustrate that the accounting and taxation implications were beyond his role and responsibility

> And, you know the accountants get involved with that as well. Cos you know there's taxation implications, so you know they can adjust those

---

96   Donald Magarey, *Buying and Selling Businesses and Companies* (Butterworths, 2nd ed, 1989) 54.

97   Participant P 2 (n 93).

numbers according to tax. You know according to the situation of the company or the vendor or the buyer.[98]

He added

> They [the vendors and the purchasers] can deal with all that stuff, you know, through their taxation and through their accountant. We don't get involved in that. We leave all that to the accountants to work all that through.[99]

**The purchaser** of a pastoral lease in the Gascoyne district said he was not familiar with the capital gains provisions and exemptions that exist under Australian law. He said he considered all animals on pastoral properties 'to be solely as tradeable stock.'[100]
He said

> Well, you know, it depends on how you want to cull. Basically, they will all be traded before they die anyway, don't they? So yeah, obviously, plant has been what's required to actually operate with machinery, fencing, water infrastructure. Whereas your livestock are basically that is what we are doing it for — is that you are breeding animals either for wool meat or otherwise. So, my understanding of the plant is, yeah, is what is required to be able to carry out that operation in the first place. [101]

In answer to the question, 'So, the stock on the station from which you breed, would you consider them still to be tradeable stock even though you are breeding with them?' He answered:

> Yes, because you know there might be a season like a dry season where you have to actually sell animals, you know what I mean? So, in the day you might sell; you might put that money away, for example, and you might buy back in once the season has improved. So, I guess at the end of the day that you know you might sell an animal and buy a replacement in later at a cheaper price. In which case, obviously, there is a profit consideration there, or otherwise there might well be a, you know, a loss in that type of transaction. [102]

---

98  Ibid.
99  Ibid.
100  Interview with Participant P 1 (Interview with Alexander Robert Fullarton, Curtin Law School, 22 December 2018).
101  Ibid.
102  Ibid.

It is noted that the scenario he gave as an example is almost identical to the facts considered in the *Wade Case*. He described his method of livestock control in reasonable detail:

> Part of the herd will be considered as breeding stock, you know, obviously you will have, say, breeding stock will be culled for age. When they are due, they will go anyway. And then obviously you will have your saleable animals which are, generally speaking, will be the offspring of your breeders anyway.
> My, the way I would operate is that obviously your female animals, you would carry them through until you cull for age. Your male animals with the example of cattle . . . you would sell them either as, you know, bulls or steers. For sheep, [that] would be [that] you would actually wether[103] them when they are younger, and so you are still going to keep your breeding stock separate to your saleable animals.[104]

His perspective was that ultimately ALL animals go to market sooner or later, so therefore, they are always considered trading stock regardless of their age.

He did make a single exception: animals kept as part of the breeding stock on the purchase and sale of pastoral properties might be considered capital, but only when transferred in association with the transfer of the entire property

> I think that's generally what you sell is to me that's what makes the operation what it is. It should be your revenue. It is where you get your income from. The only way I would consider it a capital gains type scenario is if, say, you bought animals when you bought a property with animals at a certain value and then on the sale of that property, you know what the value was at the time, but anything as far as an annual turnoff is, in my eyes, is just purely revenue. [105]

**Pastoralist two** was another person who had inherited his property, although he pointed out that despite the transfers being within the family, they involved the purchase and sale of the property. The property was formally purchased from his parents as part of a distribution of their estate. Interested parties such as siblings were entitled to their share of the estate, and parents were 'paid out' on their retirement. Hence, while the transfers were between related

---

103  Castrate.
104  Ibid.
105  Participant P 1 (n 100).

parties, the purchase and sale were reasonably close to a commercial transaction on the open market to ensure 'fair value' to all concerned.

He was aware of the distinction between breeding stock and livestock for sale but considered all livestock as trading stock. He commented that he would rather not have to sell his breeding stock but added, "well, if it's dry enough, you have to sell everything, but that has never happened to us".[106]

He said "I wouldn't put those cows on the truck unless I was forced to. Because they are more valuable to me breeding than what I can get for them."[107]

He added

> I will rarely sell a one of my better calves or cows that's within age. Because the sale price never reflects genetics effectively. If she is a cow that is breeding successfully, she's the one that I want to keep. If she's had calves every year and she'll continue to for the next few years, I will definitely be keeping her. [108]

He did not view her as trading stock and said he treated 'trade cows' and 'breeding cows' separately

> I count them as a 'Bush' cow, which means a breeding cow. Yeah. The cows that I don't want to keep I call a 'Cull' cow, and they'll be there for sale. If I call them a breeding cow, if I go through a muster and I say I draft, and I say 100 breeding cows, I say that I am definitely going to breed from in the next year.
> The ones that I don't want are spayed and some of the old ones I will spay (sterilise) them as well, and I will sell them at that moment or later when they are fatter. [109]

However, ultimately, all cattle on his property were sold. He said, 'I don't like cattle to die. I don't want them to die [on my property]. A dead cow is basically $1,000 wasted in the paddock.'[110]

---

106  Interview with Participant P 7 (Interview with Alexander Robert Fullarton, Curtin Law School, 22 July 2017).
107  Ibid.
108  Ibid.
109  Ibid.
110  Ibid.

He suggested that apart from the economic consideration of lost income, there was also an animal husbandry influence. He considered it far more humane that the animal be slaughtered in a humane fashion than perish in the heat of old age far from the nearest shade and comfort of a water hole.

He was aware that one line is classed as revenue, and the other is classed as capital gains, but he did not know a lot about it, although he had never had to sell a property.

He added the following comment

> There is a factor often overlooked by many pastoralists. It is the information of the land contained in the memory of the herd. I am talking about the knowledge that the cattle have of the land.
> I believe that it is not just a learned thing as a calf learns from its mother but I think it is somewhat genetic. It is knowledge passed from as far back as 20 generations or so.
> It is the knowledge of the land that allows the herd to prosper and develop, not merely survive and exist. It is such things as the tannin in the vegetation that can vary from morning to evening. The cow knows how the vegetation changes subtly throughout the day. Something palatable in the late afternoon might be sour in the morning.
> They not only know the lay of the land of when and where to go to for water but how to use the hills and the plains for refuge for grazing or hiding from the sun, or how to stay warm in different places or cool when it needs to. That knowledge is critical and cherished by pastoralists. Dead cattle are a lot more than just the loss of a thousand dollars that are a loss of a lot of resources — including what I call Bush knowledge.
> If you purchase cattle from other regions, they do not know how to get around on your station or the subtle difference on YOUR pasture. I have even noticed the difference when I have bought in cattle from next door. The country changes in ways that even we don't notice — but the cattle do.
> That resource is VERY precious and could never be considered by me as mere 'trading stock'; it is a capital resource and not for sale. I don't know if that is an accounting thing. I don't know much about that side of things but it is extremely important to me, and as far as I am concerned, it is a capital asset.[111]

It is noted that although stating that ultimately all cattle on his property were to be sold, pastoralist two made a clear distinction between livestock for sale as trading stock and those kept for breeding purposes as capital assets.

---

111  Ibid.

However, it is also clear that breeding stock on his property would change their status from capital assets to trading stock at the end of their 'working' life. That change of status is addressed in IAS 41. He did conclude that the classification was an accounting function and beyond his scope of expertise.

Given that the role of accountants as financial and accounting advisers has been referred to by three of the participants above, the responses of two accountants familiar with the sale of farming properties are presented.

**The rural accountant** from northern Victoria was familiar with rural sales and had been involved in finalising accounts and the preparation of income tax returns on a regular basis. But he said he had never carried out any physical inspections of properties or had direct coordination with estate agents or been asked for advice prior to the sales.

He said he had "limited input into dissecting potential sale price into tax effective categories. [His] usual involvement is for preparing tax returns only after the property sale has settled."[112]

**The urban public accountant** from Perth in Western Australia said he understood what the transaction was about and that he had prepared accounts and income tax returns for a few farms in the late 1980s and early 1990s. However, he had never been associated with the sale of a pastoral lease in the Outback.

He also said he had never been consulted as to the dissection of the sale price or how the funds had been allocated for the purchase of separate items such as plant, buildings, land, livestock and the like.

When asked if he had been consulted as to how to allocate the sale funds, he said

> No, it wasn't done that way because the sale was really dictated by the documentation, and my recollection is that the documentation treated all as trading stock by the client and also by the stock agents in selling it, and I don't recall it being separated as, you know, breeding stock x amount than number of head, as opposed to the normal trading stock. I think it was all

---

112 Interview with Participant P 5 (Telephone Interview with Alexander Robert Fullarton, Curtin Law School, 30 June 2019).

included in the one, so I suspect I would have treated it that way — following the documentation.[113]

He added:

> But had I been asked, and that was all in hindsight too, we would have seen it 12 months later after the event, and it would have been impractical to try and change the transaction well and truly after that. I wasn't asked at the beginning but I have given it some thought over the years, and I know that with some other similar type things, we have particularly made a point of separating the breeding stock in valuation and number in the contractual arrangements to the normal trading stock. That's how I believe if I was asked, that's how I would put it.[114]

It appears that despite the belief of vendors, brokers and some pastoralists that the accountants/tax preparers are consulted for their opinions on the classification and treatment of sale proceeds on the transfer of pastoral leases before and during the process of sale, they are not consulted. The examination of the broader accounting profession is beyond the scope of this research, but this book suggests that could be a topic for future research.

This study suggests that stakeholders in the ownership, transfer, administration and record keeping of animals on pastoral properties are aware of a distinction between stud or breeding stock and livestock for sale as trading stock, but ultimately, they do not account for them as such. It appears that the reliance on professional accounting advisers may be somewhat misplaced, as those advisers do not appear to be consulted in a timely fashion but are instead faced with a *fait accompli*.

It also appears that all stakeholders adopted the view that ultimately ALL livestock are sold and therefore are ALL trading stock. One pastoralist expressed that view; however, most participants considered that breeding stock should be considered as capital assets.

It appears that they may have overlooked the criteria for capital assets that says they are primarily held for more than one

---

113  Interview with Participant P 4 (Telephone Interview with Alexander Robert Fullarton, Curtin Law School, 5 June 2019).
114  Ibid.

accounting period, not that they are never disposed of. Capital assets are often eventually sold and rarely held until destruction. As the value of a capital asset is reduced over many accounting periods by way of a provision for depreciation, the sale of a capital asset can, and often does, give rise to a capital gain. Hence the concept of a capital gains tax.

This part suggests it is the complexity of recording and accounting for separating the two classifications that may be an obstacle to the distinction of some livestock being regarded as capital assets. It is simply extremely convenient, for many reasons, for stakeholders to treat ALL animals as livestock for trading purposes.

This part focuses on the definition of livestock as a capital or revenue classification, and there does not appear to be a reason suggested by accounting convention that ALL animals be classified as livestock for trading purposes. The ATO uses the case of *Federal Commissioner of Taxation v Wade*[115] to substantiate its view. A detailed examination of the *Wade Case* is conducted in Part II. It indicates that rigid adherence to the *Wade Case* to support the ATO's broader interpretation of the finding—that ALL livestock are trading stock—might be unsafe.

---

115 [1951] HCA 66; (1951) 84 CLR 105.

# PART II

# THE *WADE CASE:* AN ANALYSIS

*This part was first published as an article in the New Zealand Journal of Taxation Law and Policy in March 2021 27(2). It is re-published here mutatis mutandis with permission of the publisher.*

*It looks at the cases examined by their Honours in the Wade Case and similar cases related to the sale of livestock. It argues that the findings of the Wade Case may have been misinterpreted and that the ATO's view is not as valid as is generally accepted. It argues that the revenue from sale of stud, or breeding, animals should be taxed under the capital gains tax provisions of the ITAA 1997 and not as income according to ordinary concepts.*

# Chapter Five
# Introduction

## 5.1 Introduction

The central focus of this book is the ATO view that ALL animals sold as part of a primary production business as trading stock and that view is based on its interpretation of the decision of the *Wade Case*. The previous part of this book has examined the distinction between classifying the expenditures of an enterprise as capital (assets purchased) or revenue (costs of operation). In particular, it looks at the taxation implications of accounting for livestock as trading stock purchased, or bred, for sale and those animals purchased, or bred, for breeding purposes.

This part concludes that despite the ATO view arising from the determinations of the *Wade Case*, some animals should be classified as capital assets and therefore subject to capital gains tax (CGT). In Australia, revenue received from the sale of capital assets is provided with tax relief through certain associated exemptions and concessions. It is therefore significant to taxpayers that consideration be given to the issue that animals used for breeding purposes and sold in conjunction with a primary production business be classified as capital assets and not trading stock, as is the current view of the ATO.

Given the word ALL is not contained in s 995 of the ITAA 1997, and the Australian Tax Office (ATO) bases its interpretation solely on the findings of the *Wade Case*.[116] This part examines the decision in the *Wade Case* in greater detail than that provided in the previous part and builds on that research.

This part considers that the findings of the *Wade Case* should not be used to define all livestock as trading stock, and it should not include animals used as beasts of burden or working beasts in the business of primary production. It argues that the findings of the

---

116  Lendon (n 18).

*Wade Case* may have been misinterpreted by the ATO and that its view is not valid. Further, it not only looks at the *Wade Case* but also examines the cases considered by their Honours in the *Wade Case*, as well as similar cases relating to the sale of livestock and other business assets.

# Chapter Six
# An Analysis of the *Wade Case*

## 6.1 The Accounting Perspective

In 1951, Michael Wade was a dairy farmer carrying on business in the suburb of Osborne Park in the City of Perth, Western Australia. In the financial year 1947–48, 110 of his dairy cows were destroyed under the provisions of the *Milk Act* 1946–1947 (WA). Wade received a sum of A£2,016 (A$4,032) as compensation for the animals that were destroyed. In the same year, he purchased 116 replacement dairy cattle for the sum of A£1,986 (A$3,972).

> In his return of income for the year of income in which this took place [1948] he treated the extra six dairy cattle as a purchase of stock and showed the amount in his livestock account; but he excluded from his revenue account the receipt of £2,016 compensation for the 110 cattle condemned. Correspondingly he excluded the cost of the 110 cattle by which he replaced them, an amount of £1,886, placing a note on his return that this was a purely capital transaction.[117]

The findings detail the circumstances related to the reason the cattle were destroyed and the exact number of cattle involved. They detail the sum of compensation paid for the destroyed cattle and the number and cost of the replacement bought by Wade. However, the documents do not detail the livestock trading account furnished by Wade and amended by the Federal Commissioner of Taxation for the year of income ending 30 June 1948. Consequently, the total number of Wade's herd, the total number of cattle and their value as opening stock, and the total number of cattle and their closing value as closing stock are unavailable for scrutiny.

However, given that 110 cattle is a rather large number of cattle for a dairy farm within the environs of Perth in 1951, the severity of the disease of tuberculosis within close proximity to the population of Perth,[118] and the prevailing quarantine practices of the time,

---

117  *Wade Case* (n 1) 108–9.
118  The district of Osborne Park is now considered as an inner-city residential suburb of the city of Perth. It is 6.6 km (4 miles) from the centre of the city of Perth.

it is likely that the Chief Inspector of Stock would have required the destruction of the entire herd. That assumption is made in the suggested livestock trading account shown in Table 2.

For simplicity, Table 2 ignores all other transactions of Wade's operations. It is produced to ascertain a possible opening balance for his livestock trading account. The sums used are those provided in the findings and include the Commissioner's addition of the £2,016 receipt and the £1,886 cost of replacing the 110 cattle stated above.

Wade's amended livestock trading account in his 1948 income tax return may have appeared as follows:

**Amended Livestock Trading Account
for the year ended 30 June 1948**

| Dr | | | | Cr | | | |
|---|---|---|---|---|---|---|---|
| Date | Particulars | No. | Amount | Date | Particulars | No. | Amount |
| 1 Jul 47 | Opening stock | 110 | £1,562[119] | 14 Dec 47 | Sales | 110 | £2,016 |
| 14 Feb 48 | Purchases | 116 | £1,886[120] | 30 Jun 48 | Closing stock | 116 | £1,886 |
| | Gross profit transferred to P&L A/c | | £ 454 | | | | |
| | | 226 | £3,902 | | | 226 | £ 3,902 |
| 1 July 48 | Opening stock | 116 | £1,886 | | | | |

Table 2: Amended Livestock Trading Account.

---

119  This amount is interpolated from the sums provided in *Wade Case* (n 1) 109.
120  *Wade Case* (n 1) 106. A figure of £1,986 is disclosed at the beginning of the findings. However, the sum of £1,886 remains consistent in the balance of the findings; therefore, the sum of £1,886 is shown in this and the following livestock trading accounts.

However, as contained in the findings, the matter before the court did not consider the number of cattle or their value at the beginning of the year but rather focussed on the sum of £130 being the difference between the compensation paid (£2,016) and the expenditure of £1,886.[121]

Table 1 is provided to attempt to ascertain Wade's opening stock figures on 1 July 1947. Given that Wade did not appeal the amendment regarding the £454, it is likely that the sum of the opening stock of £1,562 is accurate, at least as to the subject cattle under scrutiny. However, any variation from that figure would render their Honours' findings to be erroneous with regard to the sum of money concerned.

Table 1 illustrates that certain assumptions were made, or relevant data was omitted, in the facts presented to the court. It illustrates that what might be an obvious mathematical conclusion in lay terms does not truly reflect the fiscal position according to accepted accounting principles. Therefore, this part considers other alternatives that may not have been considered by the court.

The findings state:

> In making his assessment for that year of income the Commissioner of Taxation **added** the £2,016 to the amount shown in Wade's return under sales and the £1,866 to the amount shown under purchases, thus increasing the assessable income derived from the livestock account by the amount of £584.[122] (emphasis added)

A detailed examination of dairy practices in Western Australia in the 1950s is beyond the scope of this research. For an understanding of the dairy industry, extensive publications are produced by Dairy Australia Ltd.[123] Relevant to this part is that in the 1950s, it was the general practice of dairy farmers to keep their cows in milk through calving.

---

121  *Wade Case* (n 1) 109. There is a discrepancy of £10 in the expenditures provided on pages 108 and 109. The finding relates to the sum of £130, which indicates that £1,886 may have been the correct figure and the sum shown on page 108 is a misprint.
122  *Wade Case* (n 1) 106.
123  Dairy Australia Ltd, *About Dairy Australia* (2019) <https://www.dairyaustralia.com.au/about-dairy-australia>.

As the calves served no purpose other than to bring the cows into milk, the pedigree of the calves was of little relevance. The resultant cross-bred weaners were disposed of as soon as possible and some sold through the livestock sale yards.[124]

It is likely that Wade may have accounted for the sale of such calves resulting from dairy operations in his livestock trading account. Based on the assumption that he had 110 cows, and each of those had one calf, the following livestock trading account is shown in Table 3.

---

124  Such inhumane practices have largely been eliminated from dairy farms in Australia. Dairy Australia Ltd, *Best Care for Animals* (2019) <https://www.sustainabledairy oz.com.au/best-care-for-animals#BestCareForAnimals>.

## Wade's Original Livestock Trading Account Option 1 for the year ended 30 June 1948

| Dr | | | | Cr | | | |
|---|---|---|---|---|---|---|---|
| Date | Partic-ulars | No. | Amount | Date | Par-ticu-lars | No. | Amount |
| 1 Jul 47 | Open-ing stock | 110 | £1,562[125] | 14 Dec 47 | Sales | 110 | £ 550[126] |
| 14 Feb 48 | Pur-chases | 6 | £ 102 | 30 Jun 48 | Clos-ing stock | 116 | £1,886 |
| 30 Jun 48 | Natural In-crease | 110 | £ 110[127] | | | | |
| | Gross profit trans-ferred to P&L A/c | | £ 662 | | | | |
| | | 226 | £2,436 | | | 226 | £ 2,436 |
| 1 July 48 | Open-ing stock | 116 | £1,886 | | | | |

Table 3: Wade's Original Livestock Trading Account Option 1.

Table 3 is a construction of Wade's livestock trading account compiled from the data provided in the findings of the *Wade Case*. Sums used reflect the assumed production of calves and the six cattle that he declared as purchases in his original income tax return.[128] The

---

125  This amount is interpolated from the sums provided in *Wade Case* (n 1) 109.

126  A fictitious figure for illustration purposes. It is assumed that if a fully grown heifer was purchased for £17, then £5 for a weaner would not be unreasonable.

127  The nearest valuation of Income Tax regulation 10(3) that could be found was in 1966. The value prescribed at that time was £1. In 1948, it may have been as little as 10/- (shillings: there were 20/- in a £); however, this figure is accepted as sufficient for illustrative purposes. Education Department of Western Australia, *Leaving Accountancy* (Technical Education Publications Trust Fund, Technical Extension Service, 1966) 415.

128  *Wade Case* (n 1) 106.

110 cattle destroyed and then replaced do not appear in the account in accordance with the findings.[129] It shows a gross profit of £662.

This part considers that sum as the original gross profit from livestock trading declared by Wade in his 1948 income tax return. The actual assessable income would have been reduced by his income from dairy operations and associated costs. However, that is beyond the scope of the findings of the court and the focus of this part.

That livestock trading account was amended by the Commissioner of Taxation. The findings state:

> In making his assessment for that year of income the Commissioner of Taxation added £2,016 to the amount shown in the livestock schedule in Wade's return under sales and the £1,886 to the amount shown under purchases, thus increasing the assessable income derived from the livestock account by £584.

Table 4 shows how the amended livestock trading account may have appeared to include his natural increase and sale of calves.

---

129  Ibid.

## Wade's Amended Livestock Trading Account Option 2
## for the year ended 30 June 1948

| Dr | | | | Cr | | | |
|---|---|---|---|---|---|---|---|
| Date | Partic-ulars | No. | Amount | Date | Par-ticu-lars | No. | Amount |
| 1 Jul 47 | Open-ing stock | 110 | £1,562[130] | 14 Dec 47 | Sales | 110 | £2,566[131] |
| 14 Feb 48 | Pur-chases | 116 | £1,886 | 30 Jun 48 | Clos-ing stock | 116 | £1,886 |
| 30 Jun 48 | Natu-ral In-crease | 110 | £ 110[132] | | | | |
| | Gross profit trans-ferred to P&L A/c | | £ 894 | | | | |
| | | 226 | **£4,452** | | | 226 | **£ 4,452** |
| 1 July 48 | Open-ing stock | 116 | £1,886 | | | | |

Table 4: Wade's Amended Livestock Trading Account Option 2.

Table 4 shows that after the amounts of £2,016 and £1,886 for the receipt of the compensation and the cost of replacement stock are added to the livestock trading account, the increase in gross profit is £232 (£894 - £662), not £584 as determined by the Commissioner in his amended assessment.

---

130  This amount is interpolated from the sums provided in *Wade Case* (n 1) 109.

131  A fictitious figure for illustration purposes. It is assumed that if a fully grown heifer is purchased for £17, then £5 for a weaner would not be unreasonable. It was raised in Wade's livestock trading account to £2,016 by their Honours when considering the transactions.

132  The nearest valuation of Income Tax regulation 10(3) that could be found was in 1966. The value prescribed at that time was £1. In 1948, it may have been as little as 10/-; however, this figure is accepted as sufficient for illustrative purposes. Education Department of Western Australia (n 20) 415.

This discussion has not been conducted to ascertain Wade's income tax liability, which was the principle focus of the *Wade Case*, but rather to illustrate that should data be examined in isolation without reference to how it fits within the broader scope of business operations, then apparently logical conclusions may not be an accurate reflection of the whole situation.

In this case, examining the additional receipt of income from the compensation paid to Wade and deducting the cost of replacement cattle (£2,016 less £1,886) to reveal an increase of £130 may be a logical mathematical conclusion, but it does not consider other factors such as the impact of the changing values of opening and closing stock, or the assigned value of natural increases.

The findings state that the average cost of closing stock was increased by £454, but the original figure is not contained in those findings. There is no way of establishing the actual opening stock value, other than the figure deduced in Table 4 (£1,562). Thus, it is noted that nearly 70 years later, a number of assumptions have to be made to estimate what the opening stock figure might have been. That those assumptions have to be made to provide a complete reconstruction of Wade's livestock trading account will be considered in the conclusion of this section.

This part focuses on the definition of livestock as a capital or revenue classification, and therefore the findings as to actual assessable income determined are beyond the scope of this research, other than to highlight that rigid adherence to *Wade* to support a broader perspective of the interpretations of the findings − ALL livestock are trading stock − might be unsafe.

## 6.2 Legislation Provisions Considered in the *Wade Case*

This section considers the definitions and interpretation of the sections of the ITAA 1936 that were the focus of the *Wade Case*. It is disclosed that to support their findings, their Honours considered s 25(c) *Income Tax Assessment Act* (1922–1934) (Cth) and ss 6(1), 26(j), 28(2), 32, 36(1) and (8) of the *Income Tax Assessment Act* (1936–1947) (Cth).

The relevant provisions are examined in the above order and compared to the findings in the *Wade Case*.

**Section 25(c)** *Income Tax Assessment Act* **(1922) (Cth)** prescribes that certain deductions not be allowed in certain cases. Section 25(c) states:

> A deduction shall not, in any case, be made in respect of: — (*c*) any loss or expense which is recoverable under any contract of insurance or indemnity;[133]

It is reported that one of the judges in the *Wade Case*, Kitto J, stated: 'Section 25(c) of the *Income Tax Assessment Act* 1922 (Cth) **allowed** a deduction in respect of any loss or expense recoverable under any contract of insurance or indemnity'[134] (emphasis added). It does not. Either the transcript is in error or his Honour was mistaken.

The relevance to this discussion is that the finding relies on the **omission** of a single word — not. The interpretation that the ATO view relies on is the **addition** of a single word — all. This part argues that the inference assumed by the omission or addition of a single word that is not contained in legislation is likely to lead to a mistaken conclusion.

The ATO view relies entirely on the inference raised by their Honours when considering the definition of livestock. 'There is a definition of livestock which, by inference, makes it clear that all animals are to be included in the case of a business of primary production.'[135] Strict adherence to the literal interpretation of that statement means that all of the horses depicted in Figure 2 are trading livestock. It would also include cattle and sheep dogs used for stock work on the farms and stations in Australia.

This examination is intended to illustrate that the reliance on a single word to express a general intent can be misleading.

**Section 6(1)** *Income Tax Assessment Act 1936* **(Cth)** defines 'livestock'. It does not define what livestock is, but rather prescribes what is not. It states it 'does not include animals used as

---

133  *Income Tax Assessment Act 1922* (Cth) s 25.
134  *Wade Case* (n 1) 115.
135  Ibid 110.

beasts of burden or working beasts in a business other than a business of primary production'.

The definition is not helpful. It has to be assumed it refers to animals. It then excludes beasts of burden and working beasts such as bullocks, donkeys, mules, camels, horses, dogs and like animals from being considered as livestock in all industries other than businesses of primary production.

That the definition predates motorisation of the transport industry is reasonably obvious. Horse-drawn vehicles were commonplace in 1915 when the Income Tax Acts were introduced into the Commonwealth of Australia. Indeed, animals were a key source of energy used on a commercial basis in Australia as late as the 1950s and remain so in some parts of the world. This section was likely intended to draw that distinction, but it ignores the function of horses and dogs in the pastoral industry.

Their Honours were not faced with the consideration of animals other than dairy cattle in the *Wade Case*. Had the concept of working animals been presented to them for consideration, they may not have been so quick as to infer 'that **all** animals are to be included in the case of a business of primary production'[136] (emphasis added).

**Section 26(j)** provides that the net revenue, if any, received by way of an insurance or indemnity in excess of the value of the loss of trading stock be assessable income. However, it permits a loss arising from an insurance recovery, in respect of any loss of trading stock shortfall, to be an allowable deduction.[137]

Kitto J referred to the application of s 26(j) in his dissenting finding and considered the surplus amount of £130 to be assessable income, despite the Commissioner of Taxation not referring to that section in his amendment of Wade's assessment.[138] However, for that section to apply, the animals had to firstly be interpreted as 'trading stock'. He confessed

---

136  Ibid.
137  *Income Tax Assessment Act 1936* (Cth) s 26(j).
138  *Wade Case* (n 1) 117.

to some difficulty in accepting the view in accepting the view that the fact
that dairy cattle, which are not trading stock according to ordinary concepts,
are required by force of a definition to be taken into account under ss 28 and
32 of the *Income Tax Assessment Act* 1936-1947 (Cth) as trading stock.

Kitto J's finding does not rely on the concept of trading stock but
rather on s 26(j), which in this case had the same outcome as the
majority findings: the surplus funds from the indemnity paid to
Wade for the loss of his dairy cattle were to be included in his assessable income.

Consequently, a firm reliance on the *Wade Case* to support the
ATO's view that ALL animals in a primary production business are
livestock for trading purposes is unsafe since only two of the three
judges accepted that inference. The third judge came to the same
finding as the other two by applying a different section of the *ITAA
1936*.

That the outcome in this case is the same is more by coinci-
dence than agreement with the preceding definition. Although
Kitto J had to first accept that the dairy cattle were presumed to be
trading stock for s 26(j) to apply, that was a concept that he had
some difficulty accepting.

**Sections 28(2), 32, 36(1) and (8)** all deal with the value of opening, closing and the natural increase (births less deaths) of trading
stock and animals as livestock for trading purposes. They apply
once it is established that ALL animals are livestock for trading purposes. Detailed discussion of those provisions is outside the scope
of this research.

In summary, in the majority findings, their Honours found
that

> Notwithstanding, therefore, the taxpayer's claim that the destruction and
> replacement of 110 head of his dairy herd is a capital transaction, it is clear
> enough that for the purposes of s 36(1) the cattle fall within the expression
> of "trading stock".[139]

Once the distinction had been made between capital expenditure,
as claimed by Wade, and revenue expenses, as found by their

---

139 Ibid.

Honours, the matter reached the conclusion that the transaction was of a revenue nature and contributed to assessable income.

That distinction was also made by the dissenting Kitto J in considering the compensation money as assessable income because they

> constitute as indemnity in respect of a loss of trading stock which would have been taken into account in computing the taxable income. Again, the definition of "trading stock", considered with the definition of livestock, brings dairy cattle within the expression[140]

and would thus fall within the provisions of s 26(j). The *ITAA 1997* s 385-130 considers compensation for loss of livestock and allows for the insurance recovery to be taken into assessable income at the rate of 20 per cent per annum. Had this option been available to Kitto J, he may well have found in favour of that alternative.

## 6.3  Cases considered in the *Wade Case*:

### 6.3.1    Commissioners of Inland Revenue v Brooks[141]

This case found that inaccuracies in estimating amendments to incomes did not operate as an estoppel against the operation of the taxing act. This finding supports the Commissioner's powers to make an amendment to Wade's assessment.

### 6.3.2    Commissioners of Inland Revenue v Newcastle Breweries Ltd[142]

It was held that the payment for rum compulsory acquired by the Admiralty 'was a profit arising from the company's trade, and that it must be included for excess profits duty purposes in the profits for the accounting period ending the 30th October, 1918, in which the rum was taken over.'[143]

---

140  *Wade Case* (n 1) 112.
141  (1915) AC 478.
142  (1927) 12 TC 927. Reported in K.BD, 42 TLR. 185, CA., 42 TLR. 609, and H.L, *43 TLR. 476.
143  (1927) 12 TC 927, 928.

As to the *Wade Case*, the matter of the insurance compensation payment being assessable for income tax purposes applies only if the receipt is considered a payment in lieu of a sale of trading stock. The finding of *Commissioners of Inland Revenue v Newcastle Breweries Ltd*[144] does not support the distinction of dairy cattle as capital assets but rather the determination of assessable income from the receipts after the distinction has been made. Those findings are not helpful in making the initial distinction, which is the focus of this part.

### 6.3.3 Commissioners of Inland Revenue v Northfleet Coal & Ballast Co.[145]

This case focussed on the manner in which a payment is made as a criterion for distinguishing between capital or revenue receipts. It was held that a lump sum payment made in lieu of periodical payments was nonetheless a revenue receipt. The payment was for product sold in the ordinary course of business. It did not bring the business to an end.

Wade did not cease business but continued to operate as a dairy with the replacement herd. The findings of *Commissioners of Inland Revenue v Northfleet Coal & Ballast Co* are not relevant to the sale of a primary production business, which terminates the business.

### 6.3.4 Commissioners of Inland Revenue v Executors of Williams[146]

Two of the judges in the *Wade Case*, Dixon and Fullagar JJ, quoted the following passage in which Lord Greene observed that:

> Not merely are the profits derived from the sale of goods in which a person trades of a revenue character, but insurance moneys received in respect of the loss of trade goods are proper receipts to appear in a revenue account. If a company insures its stock of goods against fire and that stock is destroyed by fire, however great and valuable it may be, the receipts must be treated

---

144 (1927) 12 TC 927. Reported in KBD, 42 TLR. 185, CA, 42 TLR 609, and HL, *43 TLR 476.

145 (1927) 12 TC 1102.

146 (1943) 1 All E.R. 318.

> in exactly the same manner as receipts from a sale of the goods would have been treated.[147]

That passage supports the view that insurance monies received in compensation for a loss of trading stock retain the characteristic of the asset for which the compensation was paid — in this case trading stock, and that is classified as a revenue item. Lord Greene further observed that:

> A manufacturer can, of course, insure his factory against fire. The receipts from that insurance will obviously be capital receipts. But supposing he goes further, as the manufacturer did in that case, and insures himself against the loss of profits which he will suffer while his factory is out of action.[148]

In the case of the value of a capital item compensated by an insurer, the characteristic of a capital receipt is maintained, and therefore it is not assessable income for taxation purposes.

It is only by inference that '[t]he Federal Act, however, places all animals in the category of trading stock in the case of taxpayers carrying on a business [of primary production].[149] The act does not contain the word **all**. Their Honours **inferred** that to be the case.[150] Without that inference, the findings in *Commissioners of Inland Revenue v Executors of Williams*[151] could be applied to finding the compensation paid to Wade as a capital receipt.

### 6.3.5    Danmark Pty Ltd v Federal Commissioner of Taxation[152]

This case considered the transfer of shares between related parties of a family-owned investment company. Other than to illustrate the Commissioner's powers to make an assessment, as he had done in the *Wade Case*, which is not in dispute, this part finds no relevance to the argument for the distinction between livestock for breeding purposes and livestock intended for trade.

---

147  *Commissioners of Inland Revenue v Executors of Williams* (1943) 1 All E.R. 318, 320 as quoted in *Wade*, 113.
148  *Commissioners of Inland Revenue v Executors of Williams* (1943) 1 All E.R. 318, 320.
149  *Wade Case* (n1) 113.
150  Ibid 110.
151  (1943) 1 All E.R. 318, 320.
152  (1944) 7 ATD 333.

### 6.3.6 Farnsworth v Federal Commissioner of Taxation[153]

This case considered the value of closing stock, including livestock. It found that the value of closing stock is considered assessable income. In this case, it was found that the taxpayer did not have any proprietary interest in the fruit held by a processor.

It is noted that Latham CJ stated, 'It is provided in s. 6 [ITAA 1936] that "trading stock" includes anything produced, manufactured, acquired or purchased for purposes of manufacture, sale or exchange, and also includes livestock.'[154] The statement does not include the word **all**, but Dixon and Fullagar JJ **inferred** that it did.[155] Further, Dixon and Fullagar JJ stated that in *Farnsworth v Federal Commissioner of Taxation*,[156] the matter dealt with the disposal of assets within a business and not the disposal of the entire business, and therefore s 36 did not apply.[157]

In the case study under scrutiny in this part, the matter relates to the disposal of the entire business. It is therefore suggested that the *Wade Case* cannot be relied on to support the view that ALL livestock are trading stock as the disposal of the entire business involves the disposal of animals held for breeding purposes and not only those held for trading purposes.

### 6.3.7 The Commissioners of Inland Revenue v J Gliksten & Son, Ltd[158]

The findings in *The Commissioners of Inland Revenue v J Gliksten & Son, Ltd* that

> the normal commercial method of dealing with moneys recovered by a trader under a policy of insurance, in respect of stock destroyed by fire, was to include the actual amount received in the accounts as an ordinary trading receipt in the same way as the proceeds of an ordinary sale of stock[159]

---

153  [1949] HCA 27; (1949) 78 CLR 504.
154  *Farnsworth v Federal Commissioner of Taxation* [1949] HCA 27; (1949) 78 CLR 504, 510.
155  *Wade Case* (n 1) 110.
156  [1949] HCA 27; (1949) 78 CLR 504.
157  [1949] HCA 27; (1949) 78 CLR 504, 514.
158  [1929] UKHL TC 14 364 (22 February 1929).
159  [1929] UKHL TC 14 364 (22 February 1929), 385.

support the findings in the *Wade Case* if the dairy herd is considered trading stock.

### 6.3.8    Maritime Electric Co Ltd v General Dairies Ltd[160]

This case considered a supplier of services being stopped from making a claim for a shortfall in charges arising from an error in billing systems. It was held that the supplier was not prevented from correcting the mistake and demanding payment of the difference.

As to the *Wade Case*, the Commissioner was entitled to recover the omitted taxes arising from the amendment.

### 6.3.9    The Minister for Lands v Ricketson and the Australian Mortgage, Land & Finance Co[161]

This case relates to compensation paid for the removal of a key asset — a water catchment area and a tank — from a pastoral lease. The relevance to the *Wade Case* is to indicate a definition of compensation or indemnity for the loss of the dairy cattle. Discussion of the basis for why Wade was paid is beyond the scope of this part.

The argument is that the funds paid were to compensate for a capital loss or a revenue loss. In the case of Ricketson, the finding was that the monies refunded for the term of an unexpired lease and the reduction in value to the balance of the land was held to be compensation. The classification of capital or revenue proceeds was not considered.

### 6.3.10  Short Bros., Ltd v Commissioners of Inland Revenue[162]

Short Brothers Ltd was a ship-building company. It received an order to build two steamers, but the contracts were later cancelled and £100,000 was paid to it probably to compensate for costs incurred and as compensation for loss of profits. It was subsequently taxed on that sum as to 'profits arising from any trade or business'. It supports the findings in the *Wade Case* that compensation payments

---

160  (1937) AC 610.
161  (1898) 19 LR NSW 281.
162  (1927) 12 TC 955.

form part of revenue earned from activities in the ordinary course of business.

A point of difference is that Short Brothers Ltd was in the business of building ships. Therefore, the payment in lieu of purchasing the ships is connected to the ordinary course of business. Wade was in the business of producing and selling milk, not dairy cows. This part suggests the findings in *Short Bros., Ltd v Commissioners of Inland Revenue*[163] are not helpful in making the distinction between insurance recoveries as receipts of revenue or compensation for the loss of capital assets.

### 6.3.11  Stebbing v Metropolitan Board of Works[164]

It was held in this case that the value of compensation is to rectify the value of the loss to the person from whom the property is taken, not the value to the persons acquiring the property.

The application of the findings in *Stebbing v Metropolitan Board of Works* do not appear to be directly relevant to the *Wade Case* other than to note that the value of compensation was paid through the operations of the Dairy Cattle Compensation Fund and that the monies paid to Wade were to compensate him for the slaughter of his dairy cattle.

The compensation in the *Wade Case* was marginally higher than the actual replacement of the dairy cattle. It can only be speculated whether the amended assessment would have come about if the cattle had been replaced for precisely the same value of the compensation monies received.

### 6.3.12  Van Den Berghs, Ltd v Clark[165]

In the1935 case of *Van Den Berghs, Ltd v Clark,* Lord Macmillan mentioned a number of previous cases that had illustrated the differences between monies paid in compensation for the loss of capital assets and those paid in lieu of revenue received.

---

163  (1927) 12 TC 955.
164  (1870) LR 6 QB 37.
165  (1935) AC 431, 19 TC 390.

That list, which includes most of those cases mentioned above, is referred to in the findings of the *Wade Case*. In the *Wade Case*, however, only those examples reflecting compensation for lost revenue are given. Others, which are examples of compensation for lost capital assets, such as *British Insulated & Helsby Cables, Ltd v Atherton*,[166] *John Smith & Son v Moore*,[167] *Mallett v Staveley Coal & Iron Co, Ltd*[168] and *Glenboig Union Fireclay Co, Ltd v Commissioners of Inland Revenue*,[169] are not. It is noted that Woellner et al also pointed to the characterisation of the compensation payment in *Van Den Berghs, Ltd v Clark* as being a capital payment.[170]

The omission of those alternative examples may have biased the findings of the *Wade Case*, and others that have relied on only part of Lord Macmillan's statement rather than the statement in full, which contains examples of capital assets. That may also have applied to subsequent and academic research if Lord Macmillan's statement had not been considered in its entirety.

### 6.4   Other related cases

Not considered in the *Wade Case* were the findings of Lord Normand in Kelsall Parsons & Co v Inland Revenue,[171] who also referred to the findings in Short Brothers v Commissioners of Inland Revenue and Commissioners of Inland Revenue v The Northfleet Coal and Ballast Co. He also cited those two cases when he referred to Lord Macmillan's speech in Van den Berghs, Limited, v Clark.

Lord Normand stated:

> It has been said by Lord Macmillan in *Van den Berghs, Limited, v Clark* that the question whether a particular receipt should be dealt with as an income receipt or as a capital receipt cannot be solved by reference to any provisions of the Income Tax Act, and that no infallible criterion emerges from a consideration of the case law.

---

166  [1926] AC 205.
167  [1921] 2 AC 1SC.
168  [1928] 2 KB 405.
169  [1922] SC (HL) 112.
170  Robin Henry Woellner et al, *1997 Australian Taxation Law*, (CCH Aust, 7th ed, 1997) 534.
171  [1938] SC 238.

Each case depends upon its own facts, and in this case the facts, which seem to me not to be closely analogous to the facts in any of the cases cited to us, lead me to the conclusion that the determination of the Commissioners should stand. The sum which the appellants received was, as the Commissioners have found, paid as compensation for the cancellation of the agency contract. That was a contract incidental to the normal course of the appellants' business.

I find it impossible to reconcile with some of the decided cases, for example, *Short Brothers v Commissioners of Inland Revenue*, and *Commissioners of Inland Revenue v The Northfleet Coal and Ballast Co*. These two cases were referred to by Lord Macmillan in his speech in *Van den Berghs, Limited, v Clark*, and I think they can be treated as of high authority since they passed the scrutiny of the House of Lords without adverse comment. Then it was urged that the whole structure of the appellants' business was affected by the cancellation, and that, on the authority of *Van den Berghs, Limited, v Clark*, the payment should therefore be treated as a capital payment.

However, Lord Normand found that in the case of *Kelsall Parsons & Co v Inland Revenue*[172] that the business had not ceased and that the payment should be treated as a revenue payment, and hence it was assessable income for income tax purposes.

Likewise, Wade's business did not cease, but the matter under scrutiny in this part relates to the termination of the business. It is argued that *Kelsall Parsons & Co v Inland Revenue*[173] supports the argument that as the business was cancelled, the payment should be treated as a capital payment, and the *Wade Case* is not directly relevant in this case.

Significantly, the findings of the *Robinson Case*[174] were not considered in the *Wade Case*. That case is very similar to the case in focus of this book.

> The owner of a sheep station in carrying on his business never sold or exchanged any ewes or ewe weaners off the station, but they were bred and held exclusively for breeding purposes and for their wool. The owner sold the station on a 'walk-in-walk-out' basis. Included in the sale were a number of ewe weaners.
>
> *Held*, that the ewe weaners were not "trading stock" within the definition of that term in sec. 4 of the *Income Tax Assessment Act* 1922-1925, and therefore

---

172  [1938] SC 238.
173  [1938] SC 238.
174  *Robinson Case* (n 3).

that the proceeds of the sale of such ewe weaners were not assessable income of the owner under sec. 17 (1) of that Act.[175]

If the term 'ewe' is substituted for 'cow' and 'wool' for 'milk', then the findings in *Robinson* are very similar to the circumstances in *Wade*. It is acknowledged that *Robinson's* case refers to the transfer of ownership of the entire business, as in the case study examined in this book, and that *Wade* refers only to the herd component of the business.

However, the focus of this argument is that breeding stock and trading stock are distinct concepts — capital or revenue assets. The *Robinson Case* of 1927 supports the distinction but the later *Wade Case* of 1951 does not. It may be that if the *Robinson Case* had been considered by their Honours in *Wade*, then the outcome may have been different.

It may be that the *Wade Case* focused on insurance recoveries as assessable income and substituted monies received by way of insurance recoveries as an effective sale of livestock, instead of considering the distinction between breeding stock and trading stock.

Kitto J expressed

> difficulty in accepting the view that the fact that dairy cattle, which are not trading stock according to ordinary conceptions, are required by force of a definition to be taken into account under ss. 28 and 32 of the *Income Tax Assessment Act* 1936-1947 (Cth.) as trading stock, affords a sufficient reason for bringing compensation received in respect of their compulsory destruction into the computation of taxable income.[176]

This book argues that had the findings of the *Robinson Case* been considered by his Honour, then that difficulty may have been resolved. It also looks at the issue of livestock being considered as trading stock in New Zealand. Australia and New Zealand share a common historical background and many alliances and shared interests particularly in primary production economies and trading

---

175   Ibid.
176   *Wade Case* (n1) 114.

interests.[177] As New Zealand is a farming-intensive nation, it too has addressed the matter of the classification of livestock as trading stock and therefore as a revenue rather than a capital asset.

Prebble's consideration of carrying on business in New Zealand[178] looks at the definition of livestock in the business of primary production and refers to New Zealand's landmark case of *Land Projects Limited v Commissioner of Inland Revenue* ('*Land Projects Case*').[179]

As with the *Wade Case, Land Projects Limited v Commissioner of Inland Revenue*[180] addressed the issue of the concept of livestock as trading stock. It is interesting to note that their Honours referred to the Australian *Wade Case* when making their determination that ALL livestock are trading stock.[181] One can only speculate what the outcome of *Land Projects Limited v Commissioner of Inland Revenue* might have been had the *Wade Case* found otherwise.

The Appellant argued

> that it would be ridiculous to require of a taxpayer that he should make a return of a domestic cat, a pet lamb or a favourite hunter [assume hunting dog] and therefore it could not have been intended by the Legislature in New Zealand that *all* animals should be regarded as trading stock.[182]

His Honour countered:

> I see nothing absurd in taking into account the value of a pet lamb which has grown up and turned out into the sheep farmer's regular flock so as to become an asset of the sheep farming business. A cat which is used to destroy mice in a store stacked with bags of flour may also be an asset of a business, perhaps a capital asset in ordinary bookkeeping, but it is permissible for the Legislature to declare that such an animal and many others shall for income tax purposes be deemed to be trading stock and the language of

---

177 The bond is so close that reference to New Zealand being included as a state of the Commonwealth of Australia to be formed on 1 January 1901 is found in s 6 of the *Australian Constitution*.

178 John Prebble, 'Intention to Make a Profit and "Business" in Section 65(2)(A) of the Income Tax Act 1976' (1978) 4 *Otago Law Review* 165.

179 [1964] NZLR 723.

180 Ibid 723.

181 Ibid 726.

182 Ibid 727.

subs. (1) [of s. 98] is clear. It declares that the expression "trading stock", for the purposes of s. 98 and only for those purposes, includes livestock.[183]

Of significance to this examination is that his Honour continued:

With respect, I adopt the language of Dixon and Fullagar JJ in *Wade's* case (*supra*) and say that our New Zealand Act places all animals in the category of trading stock but only of course for the purposes of s. 98.[184]

Therefore, the *Land Projects Case* does not settle the argument for New Zealand, but rather raises the speculation as to what might have been his Honour's findings had the *Wade Case* found otherwise.

However, it is also noted that the New Zealand Inland Revenue legislation considers ALL livestock as trading stock,[185] and the New Zealand Inland Revenue Department has issued a public ruling made under s 91D of the *Tax Administration Act 1994* (NZ).[186] Unlike the Australian legislation, the New Zealand legislation specifically includes livestock as trading stock.[187] It also addresses the concept of 'bloodstock' as breeding stock, but that is restricted to horses.[188]

Therefore, in New Zealand, the horses of the 'mustering crew', depicted in Part I, might not be classified as trading stock, but in Australia, the cattle dogs are.

It is noted here, and discussed in Part I, that his Honour also pointed to the accounting difficulties that may be encountered in segregating 'what portions of the sheep and cattle at Happy Valley were held only for breeding purposes and what portions were held merely until such time as they should be ready for sale.'[189]

---

183  Ibid.
184  Ibid.
185  *Income Tax Act 2007* (NZ) s YA 1; (definition of 'trading stock').
186  New Zealand Inland Revenue Department, Tax Technical, ' Income Tax — Timing of Disposal and Derivation of Income from Trading Stock' BR PUB 14/08 (30 September 2014) https://www.taxtechnical.ird.govt.nz/-/media/project/ir/tt/pdfs/rulings/public/pu14008.pdf?la=en.
187  *Income Tax Act 2007* (NZ) s YA 1.
188  Ibid.
189  *Income Tax Act 2007* (NZ) s YA 1.

This book argues that 56 years later and with the advent of electronic data processing, which did not exist in 1964, those difficulties are no longer the obstacles they once were. It now moves on to Part III to investigate the background to the *Wade Case* from source documents not reported in the decision of the case to seek insight of events leading to Wade's tax assessment and subsequent appeals. The investigation reveals facts never considered by the High Court.

# PART III

# THE FOUNDATIONS OF THE *WADE CASE*: CONCRETE OR CLAY?

*This part was first published as an article in the Journal of Australian Taxation in December 2022 24(1). It is re-published here mutatis mutandis with permission of the publisher.*

*This part investigates unreported documentary evidence as background to the Wade Case and compares them with earlier parts of this book and previous publications to provide deeper insight of the case and to address some of the earlier assumptions.*

# Chapter Seven
# Introduction

## 7.1 Introduction

This part argues that the Australian Taxation Office (ATO) practice of issuing opinions and taxation rulings for the guidance of taxation practitioners compiling and submitting taxation returns does not always result in greater clarity or certainty in the application of taxation laws. To illustrate that argument this part addresses the example wherein the ATO considers all animals used in a business of primary production as trading stock. However, as previously stated, the word all is not contained in s 995 of the Income Tax Assessment Act 1997 (Cth) (ITAA 1997); but rather, the ATO view is based on its interpretation of the findings in the appeal case of the *Wade Case*.

However, it has been previously argued that dairy cattle, and stud stock held for breeding purposes, should be treated as capital assets and not trading stock. Previous parts examined the *Wade Case* but contained a number of assumptions made due to a lack of substantiable evidence. Subsequent investigation of the High Court appeal books and other documentary evidence focusing on initial Commonwealth Taxation Board of Review decision that preceded the Commissioner of Taxation's appeal to the High Court is examined in this part. This part analyses those documents and investigates background not reported in Court authorised publications. It compares them with previous parts to reveal a deeper insight of the case and addresses the assumptions made in those publications. It argues that the *Wade Case* focused on the assessable nature of monies received as compensation for loss of assets. That Wade's loss was dairy cattle is somewhat irrelevant to the findings of the case. This part finds that, prior to 1936, animals used as breeding stock were of capital nature for taxation purposes. However, the legislation making that distinction was repealed in 1936. That amendment rendered all animals used in a business of primary production to be classified as trading stock. Therefore, it concludes that while ATO view is correct, the basis supporting the view is not.

Broadly, this part argues that rulings, determinations and advice provided by the ATO should not be considered by tax practitioners as always providing for greater clarity and certainty in the preparation and lodgement of taxation returns and the payment of tax. The practice of accepting the ATO opinion unchallenged can have extremely significant fiscal impacts on taxpayers and tax collections. To illustrate those impacts, this part uses a hypothetical case study provided in chapter three as to the sale of a pastoral lease by the executor of a deceased estate.

That hypothetical case study reveals that the discrepancy of tax payable by considering the cattle remaining on the pastoral lease for breeding purposes capital assets rather than as livestock for sale is considerable. Animals left on the pastoral lease by the Executor for the purpose of maintaining a breeding herd at an estimated value of AUD 300 000 and attract an income tax liability of around AUD 50 000. However, by considering breeding or stud animals as capital assets then, after capital gains tax concessions, the tax liability is reduced to nil. This part suggests that for want of thorough research and challenge of 'accepted' principles, taxpayers have over paid a significant sum of tax to the ATO as income has been wrongly assessed.

However, it must be noted that the ATO may not be directly responsible for the anomaly. While it has provided guidance on its view, the ATO clearly states as a caveat that its opinion may not be correct, and its written opinions include a specific disclaimer that states:

> If this advice turns out to be incorrect and you underpay your tax as a result, you will not have to pay a penalty. Nor will you have to pay interest on the underpayment provided you reasonably relied on the advice in good faith. However, even if you don't have to pay a penalty or interest, you will have to pay the correct amount of tax.[190]

---

190  Lendon (n 18).

Tax agents are duty bound to take reasonable care to ensure that taxation laws are applied correctly to the circumstances in relation to which they are providing advice to a client,[191] and in that context this book asserts that agents should not simply accept that the ATO's view on a matter necessarily represents the correct view of an issue.

Chapter four notes that, despite the ATO's caveat that its advice could be incorrect, the majority of accountants, tax practitioners and other professionals involved in the sale of pastoral leases considered that in order to be in compliance with the tax accounting requirements, establishing the distinction between livestock as breeding stock and those as trading stock should be carried out, but ultimately, it is too hard; hence, the livestock trading account (revenue) option is adopted. That is despite most of them being aware of the CGT concessions.

This book suggests that tax practitioners should use such ATO rulings and determinations as a guide but not as a rigid matter of law. Each case should be considered on its merits and assessed accordingly. However, in the example addressed in this part, which refers to the use of the *Wade Case* as concrete evidence to determine a particular class of asset, it appears that many hundreds of taxpayers may have paid many millions of dollars in tax over a period of over 70 years, as the opinion of the ATO has been accepted without challenge.

This part examines the view held by the ATO that *all* animals held in a business of primary production are trading stock for the purposes of sale, regardless of their actual purpose or function in that business. That view appears counter intuitive to people with a rural background or familiarity with farming. It might appear nonsensical to consider the horses and dogs used to muster sheep and cattle form part of the trading stock of a farm which produces animal products such as wool or milk. One does not normally shear or milk horses and dogs, but the ATO view considers them as trading stock — a revenue assets, rather than as aids to manufacture or as plant — a capital asset.

---

191  Code of Professional Conduct *Tax Agent Services Act 2009* (Cth) s 30-10.

A broad examination of the ATO view is contained in the previous chapters. The previous parts of this book challenged the ATO's view and argued that stud stock, or animals used for breeding or other purposes, are not trading stock but rather should be considered as capital assets used for the purposes of manufacture. The previous parts argued that the word *all* is not contained in s 995 of the *Income Tax Assessment Act 1997 (ITAA 1997)*, but found that the ATO view relies entirely on the rulings in the *Wade Case* for support. However, no taxation ruling, determination or other public notice could be found that contained that view, other than an Interpretative Decision,[192] which focuses on considering animal embryos are not to be livestock, therefore ATO advice was sought to confirm that view. The advice received[193] acknowledged the taxation legislation does not contain the word *all* in its definitions of livestock and confirmed that ATO view and that the Commissioner of Taxation relies on the findings of the *Wade Case* to substantiate the view 'that the definition of livestock in section 995-1 of the *ITAA 1997* includes all animals in a primary production business'.[194]

Given that the Commissioner's view relies entirely on the *Wade Case*, which has had a significant impact on the amount of tax paid by Australian primary producers over the past 70 years, an examination of the *Wade Case* was conducted to investigate and evaluate the reliability of the decisions that were given in support his opinion.

Part II found that sufficient doubt existed to suggest that the Commissioner's view might not be reliably supported by the decision of the *Wade Case*. It further supported the argument that some animals held in a business of primary production, such as horses and dogs used for mustering and stud stock used for breeding, or the production of animal products such as milk or wool, are of a capital nature and should be treated accordingly for taxation purposes.

---

192  Australian Taxation Office, *Income Tax: Definition of Livestock and Animal Embryos* (ID 2003/726, 30 July 2003).
193  Lendon (n 18).
194  Ibid.

Part I examined the distinction between classifying the expenditures of an enterprise as capital (assets purchased) and classifying them as revenue (costs of operation), and, in particular, they looked at the taxation implications of accounting for livestock as trading stock purchased, or bred, for sale rather than as purchased, or bred, for breeding purposes.

It argued that animals kept for breeding purposes are capital assets, and therefore the proceeds of the sale of those animals, in conjunction with the sale of the property and other assets contained thereon for the purpose of operating the business, are capital sales. Thus, that proportion of the proceeds of the sale of the primary production business should be subject to the [capital gains tax] (CGT) provisions [of the ITAA 1997] and taxed accordingly.

It is also noted that the advice received from the ATO contained reference to the ATO Interpretative Decision ID 2003/726. It is significant that the ID 2003/726 also recognises that the word *all* is not contained within s 995 of the *ITAA 1997*, but refers to the 'inference' in the decisions of the *Wade Case* that all animals that are used in primary production are included in the definition of livestock.

In particular the advice from the ATO refers to part of the decision in the *Wade Case* as follows:

> Rather than outlining what is considered to be livestock this definition merely states which animals are not considered to be livestock. However, in *Federal Commissioner of Taxation v. Wade* (1951) 84 CLR 105; (1951) 9 ATD 337; (1951) 5 AITR 214 (*Wade's Case*), the High Court considered that this definition infers that all animals that are used in primary production are included in the definition of livestock. Per Dixon and Fullagar JJ:
> There is a definition of livestock which, by inference, makes it clear that all animals are to be included in the case of a business of primary production.[195]

Therefore, this part also considers the ATO advice that the statement in the decision of the *Wade Case* that the definition of livestock 'by inference, makes it clear that all animals are to be included in the case of a business of primary production'[196] is sufficient to

---

195  Lendon (n 18).
196  Ibid.

substantiate the opinion that NO animals held in a business of primary production can be considered as capital assets used for the purposes of producing saleable goods, but rather that *all* animals used in a business of primary production ARE saleable goods, that is trading stock.

In 1950 Michael Wade appealed to the Commonwealth Taxation Board of Review (CTBR) to set aside an amendment made by the Commissioner of Taxation to his 1948 income tax return. The matter found in favour of the taxpayer, and the decision was subsequently appealed to the Australian High Court by the Commissioner of Taxation in 1951.[197] The Full Bench of the Australian High Court allowed the Commissioner's appeal, and the decision of the Board of Review was set aside.

This part looks beyond the decision of the full bench of the High Court and conducts further research into the background of the *Wade Case* by way of examining the initial decision in Wade's earlier appeal to the CTBR[198] and the Commissioner's initial appeal to the High Court.[199] Therefore, in order to fill in the gaps in the previous research and to support, or refute, the findings of the previous parts, this part examines the evidence presented to the CTBR as the background to the *Wade v Commissioner of Taxation*[200] decision. It also examines commentary of other reports of the CTBR matter such as Butterworth's *Commonwealth Taxation Board of Review Decisions*[201] and Wolters Kluwer's *CCH Taxation Board of Review Decisions*.[202]

---

197  *Wade Case* (n 1).

198  *Wade v Commissioner of Taxation*, Commonwealth Taxation Board of Review No. 2. (1950) No M37/1950. Note: The matter is also reported as (1950) 1 CTBR (NS) Case 77, 335; and (1950) 1TBRD Case 72, 273.

199  *Commissioner of Taxation v Wade* (High Court of Australia, Kitto J. 4 September). It should be noted that the matter was initially heard by Kitto J alone on 4 September 1951. A decision was not made at that time, but rather it was ordered that the case should be argued before the Full Bench of the High Court.

200  *Wade v Commissioner of Taxation* (n 198).

201  John Angus Lancaster Gunn and Richard Esmond O'Neill (eds), *Commonwealth Taxation Board of Review Decisions (New Series)* (Butterworth and Co, 1952) 1; (1 CTBR (NS)).

202  Wolters Kluwer, CCH Australia *CCH iKnow* (online at 2 April 2022).

The following section re-examines the *Wade Case* in detail, with the further evidence produced to the High Court arising from the CTBR case of *Wade v Commissioner of Taxation* and the first appeal by the Commissioner to the High Court.[203] It also re-examines the previous parts to address the gaps in the earlier analyses.

---

203 *Commissioner of Taxation v Wade* (n 199).

# Chapter Eight
## The *Wade Case* Revisited

## 8.1 Background

The previous analysis of the decision of the *Wade Case* gave the following overview of the case and the details known at that time namely that:

In 1951, Michael Wade was a dairy farmer carrying on business in the suburb of Osborne Park in the City of Perth, Western Australia. In the financial year 1947–48, 110 of his dairy cows were destroyed under the provisions of the *Milk Act* 1946–1947 (WA). Wade received a sum of A£2,016 (A$4,032) as compensation for the animals that were destroyed. In the same year, he purchased 116 replacement dairy cattle for the sum of A£1,986 (A$3,972).

In his return of income for the year of income in which this took place [1948] he treated the extra six dairy cattle as a purchase of stock and showed the amount in his livestock account; but he excluded from his revenue account the receipt of £2,016 compensation for the 110 cattle condemned. Correspondingly he excluded the cost of the 110 cattle by which he replaced them, an amount of £1,886, placing a note on his return that this was a purely capital transaction.[204]

The following sequence of events has been compiled from the documents contained in the Appeal Book provided to the judges in the *Wade Case*. The documents not only contain a timeline of the events leading to the Commissioner of Taxation's appeal to the full court of the High Court of Australia, but also provide an insight into the facts and points of Law considered by their Honours but not written into the reported decision of the case.[205]

---

204 *Wade Case* (n 1) 108–9.
205 The High Court of Australia authorises its decisions to be published in the Commonwealth Law Reports 1903-(CLR) by Westlaw Australia and the Australasian Legal Information Institute; Gunn and O'Neill (n 201).

## 8.2 Timeline of events

**13 May 1949** Michael Wade lodged his return of income for the financial year ended 30 June 1948. Of significance to this matter is that he excluded the financial transactions relating to the destruction and replacement of 110 cattle held in his primary production business. However, a note was included in his tax return disclosing the event but stating that the transactions were not disclosed as income as they were of a capital nature and did not form part of Wade's assessable income.[206]

**26 August 1949** The Commissioner of Taxation issued his assessment of taxation to Wade based on his income tax return, but adjusted to include the transactions relating to the disposal and replacement of the 110 cattle.[207]

**13 September 1949** Wade objected to the assessment on three grounds —

1.  'Cattle condemned and replaced from the compensation paid should not enter the trading stock of cows at all.'
2.  Milk consumed assessed at the value of £26 was excessive. And
3.  The reduction of 'Amount expended on food for employees' from £1 per head per week to 15/- was wrong. The original sum of £1 per head per week should be used.[208]

**18 October 1949** The Deputy Commissioner of Taxation for Western Australia notified Wade that his objection was disallowed and that he could refer the matter to a Board of Review, or appeal to the High Court or to the Supreme Court of a State. The notice further advised Wade of the requirement for the payment of a fee of £1 to accompany a request to a tribunal.[209]

---

206  *Commissioner of Taxation v Wade* Appeal Book High Court of Australia, 9 of 1950, 18.
207  Ibid 14.
208  Ibid 24-6. Note the symbols £ and /- are for Australian Pounds Sterling and Shillings. Prior to 14 February 1966 Australia used the British Sterling system of currency in which a pound consisted of 20 shillings.
209  Ibid 27-8.

**14 November 1949** Wade advised the Deputy Commissioner of Taxation (WA) of his request to have the matter referred to the Board of Review, and paid the £1 prescribed fee.[210]

**19 May 1950** The Second Commissioner of Taxation referred Wade's request for a decision on the objection to his assessment to the Taxation Board of Review No. 2 in Melbourne.[211]

The request was accompanied by a statement that the Commissioner's reasons for disallowing the taxpayer's claims were—

1.  That the taxpayer disposed of part of assets of his business being trading stock and the amount of £2 016 is, pursuant to section 36(1) of the Income Tax Assessment Act 1936-1948, assessable income;
    alternatively,
    the amount of £2,016 was received as or by way of insurance or indemnity and is assessable income under the provisions of section 26(j) of that Act.
2.  That the value of produce taken from the business and used for the maintenance of the taxpayer and his employees was not less than £26.
3.  That the expenditure incurred by the taxpayer in providing food for his employees was not greater than £270.[212]

That statement is not helpful unless Wade's income tax return and assessment are considered, so that the points of discrepancy.

1.  Wade had not included the £2016 compensation payment in his income tax return, but rather had appended a note:

| | | |
|---|---|---|
| 110 | Cattle condemned by Stock Department. | |
| | Received Compensation. | 2016 |
| 110 | Cattle replacement cost | 1886 |
| Purely a Capital transaction.[213] | | |

---

210  Ibid 29.
211  Ibid 30.
212  Ibid 31-2.
213  Note appears to have been glued to page 3 of the income tax return 'LIVE STOCK SCHEDULE. Ibid 18.

2.  Drawings of goods for own use cannot be located on the income tax return.[214] It is assumed that there was a nil declaration and the Commissioner adjusted the assessment by the entire £26; and
3.  Wade claimed £1 per week per employee for food, giving a total of £360. The Commissioner adjusted that expenditure to 15/- per week per employee, or £270.

In total, the Commissioner had increased Wade's assessable income by £2589 from £5025 to £7614.[215]

The Commissioner had also increased Wade's allowable deductions by £1780 from £3886 to £5666. The result was a net increase in taxable income from £1140 to £1948.[216]

It should be noted that in 1948, £808 was a considerable sum of money for a small dairy farmer on the outskirts of Perth in Western Australia, especially one who had just suffered the misfortune of having his entire dairy herd slaughtered as a quarantine measure to prevent the spread of tuberculosis. By comparison, the average male income was just £7/17/6 ($15.75) a week or £409/10 ($819) a year.[217] In modern times the argument over the adjustment to Wade's taxable income may appear paltry, but in 1948 it was significant.

**12 September 1950** Wade's evidence was put to the Taxation Board of Review, with examination by W E Southwood (representing Wade) and cross-examination by Edward Thomas C Cain (representing the Commissioner). A transcript of the proceedings was included in the Appeal Book provided to their Honours in the subsequent appeal to the Full Bench of the High Court.[218]

The outcome was that Wade withdrew two of the three claims disallowed by the Commissioner, namely numbers two and three (relating to goods drawn for his own use and the value of the employees' meals). The first, and remaining claim, was in respect of

---

214  Ibid 16-20.
215  Ibid 22.
216  To further complicate the analysis Wade had also declared £1 of property income.
217  ABS Cat 6350.0.
218  *Commissioner of Taxation v Wade* (n 199) 33-8.

whether the compensation for and replacement of the dairy cattle should be excluded from the taxpayer (Wade's) assessable income, save for the £130 difference between the compensation paid (£2016) and the cost of the replacement of 110 cattle (£1886). The remainder, the £454 (the value of the closing stock), was to be considered as assessable income.[219]

**8 December 1950** The Commissioner of Taxation lodged a notice of appeal to the High Court to resolve the following questions of law:

1.  Whether the condemnation and killing of the said cattle and the receipt of £2,016 as compensation was a disposal of trading stock within the meaning of section 36 of the Income Tax Assessment Act 1936-1948;
2.  Whether the said sum of £2,016 was an amount received by the Respondent by way of insurance or indemnity for or in respect of any loss of trading stock which would have been taken into account in computing assessable income within the meaning of section 26(j) of the Income Tax Assessment Act 1936-1948; and
3.  Whether the Board of Review was right in holding that it was not open to it to find that the said amount of £2,016 could have been included under section 26(j) of the Income Tax Assessment Act 1936-1948.[220]

**4 September 1951** The Commissioner of Taxation appealed to the High Court before a single judge, Kitto J, to lodge an appeal to the Full Bench of the High Court.[221] Evidence was presented by N A Lappin for the Commissioner, with Edward Thomas C Cain as witness for the appellant. The order was 'that this case be argued

---

219  Ibid 39-61.
220  Ibid 14. It is noted that the Commissioner of Taxation might have appealed to the Western Australian Supreme Court in the order of the hierarchy of courts. Since 1977 the matter might have been appealed to the Federal Court, as it refers to Commonwealth legislation; however, it was not, and was referred initially to a single judge of the High Court. The decision to refer the matter to the Full Bench was made by Kitto J.
221  Ibid 2-9.

before a Full Court at the present sittings of the Court in Perth'[222] and that 'the transcript of these notes will be available for the members of the Full Court'.[223]

**10 September 1951** The Commissioner's appeal was referred by Kitto J in Perth Western Australia to the Full Bench of the High Court.[224]

**5 November 1951** The Commissioner's appeal was heard in Melbourne by the Full Bench of the High Court.[225] It should be noted that the Full Bench included Kitto J, who had heard the initial appeal and had had the benefit of hearing Wade's and the Commissioner's evidence in the Court.[226]

It should also be noted that N A Lappin appeared for the Commissioner of Taxation, but there was no appearance of counsel for the respondent. Dixon and Fullagar JJ noted that 'There was no appearance upon the appeal for the respondent taxpayer',[227] and assumed that the taxpayer 'doubtless regarded the amount of the consequential reduction of tax as insubstantial'.

However, the transcript of the proceedings before Kitto J on 4 September contains a discussion as to why neither Michael Wade nor his solicitors would be attending the appeal hearing and an undertaking by N A Lappin 'to see that a copy of [the] notes will be available for the members of the Full Court'.[228] The transcript also contains a confirmation of an undertaking that the Commissioner would not apply for an order for costs against the taxpayer.[229]

No transcript of the hearing before the Full Bench was found for this research, and the decision in that matter relies entirely on the publication found in the *Commonwealth Law Reports*. However, this part considers the background evidence put in the *Wade Case*, therefore a verbatim record of proceedings might be considered

---

222  Ibid 9.
223  Ibid.
224  Judges Dixon, Fullagar and Kitto.
225  *Wade Case* (n 1).
226  Transcript of proceedings before his Honour Mr Justice Kitto 4 September 1951 *Commissioner of Taxation v Wade* (n 199) 2-9.
227  *Wade Case* (n 1) 338.
228  *Commissioner of Taxation v Wade* (n 199) 9.
229  Ibid 7.

beyond the scope of this research, but would have been examined if available. The observation as to representation and costs above, is not intended to imply a negative assessment of their Honours' observations, which are obiter dictum or simply an expression of their opinion, but rather to illustrate details which may have been overlooked in the reported decision.

A central tenet of this part is that reliance on the decision published in the *Commonwealth Law Reports*, while they are accepted as supporting evidence for an argument before the court, may not be sufficient to provide a concrete base for all similar matters, as the ATO advice may imply. It is also noted that the ATO advice contains a disclaimer to the effect that the advice could subsequently be proved to be incorrect. The small matter outlined above supports the argument of this book. Wade did not appear, nor did his counsel, as it was previously undertaken by the Crown Solicitor that Wade's evidence would be put to the Full Bench and that costs would not be sought by the Commissioner against Wade. He had no need to journey to Melbourne to give the same evidence that he had given in Perth before Kitto J. Kitto J was aware of this, but it appears that the other judges were not.

## 8.3 Taxation Review Board Evidence Applied

Part II examined the High Court's decision in the *Wade Case*, but those examinations were limited in that they relied on the reported decisions of the High Court[230] and a number of assumptions had to be made, such as the actual livestock trading beyond the destruction and replacement of the 110 cattle which were the focus of the case.

When writing Part II, the evidence provided to the Taxation Board of Review was not found.[231] However, the Appeal Book

---

230  *Wade Case* (n 1).
231  It is noted that 'in Australia, there are many other official bodies though [they are] not courts. These bodies are sometimes said to be performing a 'quasi-judicial' function. Decisions of administrative tribunals are sometimes reported in much the same way as court decisions.' (Catriona Cook et al., *Laying Down the Law* (Butterworths, 5th ed, 2001) 82). However, cases may not be reported and the record of *Wade v Commissioner of Taxation Board of Review No. 2* (1950)

copies provided to the High Court generally, and to Kitto J specifically, include the decision of the Taxation Board of Review, the statement of reasons supporting that decision and other documents given in evidence by the Commissioner of Taxation and Michael Wade to the Board.

Part II found that Dixon and Fullagar JJ accepted the concept that the cattle were to be considered trading stock, and therefore of a revenue nature, irrespective of the role that they played in the business. It also noted that Kitto J was reluctant to accept that principle, but focused instead on the concept of insurance recoveries and the costs of repairs to support his decision.[232]

Part II also pointed to a number of relevant previous cases that were not considered by the High Court. Without supporting documentation other than the report published in the *Commonwealth Law Reports* it could not be concluded whether their Honours were aware of those cases, or if they had been omitted from either the evidence or the reported decisions. The evidence provided by the Appeal Books reveals that those other cases were not put to the High Court for consideration.[233]

Further, the Board heard substantive evidence that Wade had suffered greatly from the loss of his existing herd of cows, and that the replacements were not a 'like-for-like' exchange. Wade pointed to 'extra labour in bringing them in and getting the quiet which was a very hard task and they were not the same class of milkers as I had had on the property for many years.'[234] None of these 'non-fiscal' considerations can be found in the *Commonwealth Law Report*

---

was discovered in the copy of the Appeal Book — copy of his Honour Mr Justice Kitto (*Wade Case* (n 1)).

232   Ibid.

233   For example: The *Robinson Case* (n 3) held that ewe weaners were not trading stock as they were held for the purposes of breeding and that the proceeds of the sale of such ewe weaners were not assessable income. However, it has been found that s 17 of the ITAA 1922, in force at the time, expressly excluded livestock, which in the opinion of the Commissioner, Assistant Commissioner or Deputy Commissioner, are ordinarily used as beasts of burden or as working beasts or for breeding purposes. (Part II).

234   *Commissioner of Taxation v Wade* (n 201) 34.

publication, as the report focuses on the decision and not on the evidence presented to the court.

It should also be noted that, in Australia, administrative tribunals are not judicial bodies and may function in a less formal manner than the 'Judicature'. The decisions of Australian tribunals focus on fairness and equity rather than on a strict application of the law. Courts may set aside the decisions of tribunals for a number of reasons, but not if it is unreasonable to do so.[235] That discrimination is significant to the background of this case, as what may have been determined by the Board to be fair as a matter of equity or social inequality, may not have been in accordance with a literal approach to legislative interpretation or the 'Black-Letter Law' as adopted by the High Court in 1951.[236]

Part II concluded that a number of changes have been made in the past 71 years in the approach to legal interpretation which may have significant impact on the outcome of a modern challenge to the decision of the *Wade Case*. It that:

> The *Wade Case* of 1951 relies substantially on British cases for precedent. In 1951, the British courts were courts of appeal for Australian cases. British court findings have not bound Australian courts since 1986;[84] therefore, the precedents set by those cases, which bound the High Court in 1951, no longer apply. It is argued that if the *Wade Case* were held in modern times, the outcome may be somewhat different.
> Further, since the *Wade Case* of 1951, capital gains tax has been introduced (1985) and the Asprey Report of 1975 indicated that livestock could be considered capital assets rather than trading stock. In addition, the introduction of accounting standards relating to biological assets since 2000 indicate that the ATO view may not be as relevant in 2020 as it was before those events.[237]

A significant development in the approach to legislative interpretation is the enactment of s 15AA of the *Acts Interpretation Act 1901* (Cth) in 1981,[238] which prescribes that:

---

235  Commonwealth of Australia, Administrative Appeals Tribunal, 'Tribunals in Australia: Their Roles and Responsibilities' (Web Page) <https://www.aat.gov.au/about-the-aat/engagement/speeches-and-papers/the-honourable-justice-garry-downes-am-former-pres/tribunals-in-australia-their-roles-and-responsibilities>.

236  Cook et al. (n 231) 208.

237  *Australia Act 1986* (Cth).

238  Statute Law Revision Act 1981 (Cth) no. 61, 1981 - schedule 1.

> In interpreting a provision of an Act, the interpretation that would best
> achieve the purpose or object of the Act (whether or not that purpose or ob-
> ject is expressly stated in the Act) is to be preferred to each other interpreta-
> tion.[239]

Therefore, unbound by the restrictions of a literal interpretation
that infers that *all* animals are to be included in the case of a business of primary production,[240] their Honours may have looked at
the purpose to which the cattle were put as aids to manufacture.
They may have considered that the legislation did not intend to
capture animals used as aids to manufacture but just animals actu-
ally used as trading stock for the purposes of making a profit. However, a detailed investigation of the outcome of the *Wade Case* has
been addressed in Part II and is beyond the scope of this part.

The focus of this part is to examine the evidence leading to the
appeal to the Full Bench of the High Court of Australia, the final
court of appeal used by the Commissioner of Taxation in this matter.[241] Therefore, it moves on to examine the decision of the Taxation
Board of Review and the evidence put to the High Court. It also
introduces information not previously considered in Part II, such as
Wade's actual livestock trading account filed in his 1948 income tax
return that was amended by the Commissioner of Taxation.

## 8.4 Analysis of the Taxation Board of Review documents and the transcript of proceedings

This analysis compares the research presented in Part II to the evidence presented to the Taxation Board of Review and the Board's
decision, with the transcript of proceedings of the first hearing of
the High Court before Kitto J in Perth on 4 September 1951.[242] In the
absence of detailed information, the authors made assumptions as
to the accounting treatment of Wade's dairy herd for the fiscal year

---

239 *Acts Interpretation Act 1901* (Cth) s 15AA.
240 *Wade Case* (n 1) 110.
241 Australian appeals were abolished by a gradual, and messy, legislative process
   that began in 1968 and ended with the Australia Act 1986 <https://www.hcour
   t.gov.au/assets/publications/speeches/former-justices/gleesoncj/cj_18jun08.
   pdf>.
242 Transcript of Proceedings (n 226).

ended 30 June 1948 and what the livestock trading account may
have shown in his 1948 income tax return. Part II states:

> The findings detail the circumstances related to the reason the cattle were
> destroyed and the exact number of cattle involved. They detail the sum of
> compensation paid for the destroyed cattle and the number and cost of the
> replacement bought by Wade. However, the findings do not detail the live-
> stock trading account furnished by Wade and amended by the Federal Com-
> missioner of Taxation for the year of income ending 30 June 1948.

However, the *Commonwealth Taxation Board of Review (New Series)*
contains a 'summarised result of the [Commissioner's] alterations
as regards [Wade's] cattle'[243] which is an excerpt of Wade's
amended livestock trading account. It is noted that the existence of
two authorised court reporting publications may assist researchers
in their examination of previous cases and an examination of both
reports may be warranted to reveal detail not contained in one or
the other. It is also noted here that the preamble presented in the
Australasian Tax Decisions[244] version report of the decision of the
*Wade Case* contains a detailed reproduction of the Commissioner's
calculations to the adjustments of the Live Stock Schedule to arrive
at a trading profit of £584, after considering the 'sale' and 'purchase'
of the dairy herd and the impact on the average value of the closing
stock. The Commonwealth Law Report version does not. The Commonwealth Law Report version contains the same detail, but in
word form rather than set out in an accounting form.

In this example examination of both publications might have
assisted the examination in Part II. Detailed discussion of the impacts of the existence of two publications is beyond the scope of this
book but might be considered in future research. Detail of the livestock trading account furnished by Wade in his 1948 income tax return was not found by the authors. However, it is contained in the
copy of Wade's 1948 income tax return contained in the certified
copy of the Appeal Book[245] and is reproduced in Table 5.

---

243  Gunn and O'Neill (n 201) (1950) 1 CTBR (NS) Case 77, 339.
244  The *Australian Tax Decisions* (ATD) series contains Australian tax cases from
     1930 to 1969. The ATD series was originally published in 15 volumes by the
     Law Book Company. It was sometimes known as Australasian Tax Decisions.
245  Part of Wade's 1948 income tax return is contained in Kitto J's Appeal Book, but
     several pages, including the Live Stock Schedule, are missing.

## Live Stock Schedule
## for the year ended 30 June 1948

| Dr | Column A | | | Column B | | Cr | |
|---|---|---|---|---|---|---|---|
| Date | Particu-lars | No. | Amount | Date | Particu-lars | No. | Amount |
| 1 Jul 47 | Opening stock: Cattle Horses | 94 9 | £ 748 68 | | Sales: Cattle Horses | 24 3 | £ 208 8 |
| | Pur-chases: Cattle Horses | 24 6 | £ 356 5 | | Deaths: Horses | 3 | |
| | Natural In-crease: Cattle | 20 | | 30 Jun 48 | Closing stock: Cattle Horses | 114 10 | £ 929 95 |
| | | 153 | £ 1247 | | | 153²⁴⁶ | £ 1240 |

Table 5: Wade's 1948 Live Stock Schedule.

The structure of the Live Stock Schedule does not follow modern accounting standards of a Livestock Trading Account however the net loss of £7 is contained in Part D of the 1948 income tax return under 'Income as Farmer, Pastoralist, Horticulturist etc.'[247] The total of Column A is shown in item 43 as income from sales and the total of Column B is shown in item 46 as a deduction from that income. Hence the Live Stock Schedule does not balance with the profit and loss as transferred to the Profit and Loss account, as it would in the presentation of a modern set of accounting statements, which was assumed in Part II.

Table 5 bears little resemblance to the Livestock Trading Account proposed in Part II shown below in Table 6. The discrepancy indicates the danger of making assumptions from part records presented in authorised law reports of decisions. This book suggests

---

246 There is a mathematical error in that the total of the column is 154 not 153 as shown. It is noted that there are a number of mathematical errors throughout the income tax return and the Commissioner's amendments. The court decision noted the errors and adjusted them accordingly. Therefore, these did not influence the ultimate outcome of the case.

247 *Commissioner of Taxation v Wade* (n 199) 17.

that, for a more accurate legal analysis, the evidence submitted to the court and transcripts of the hearings should be consulted as well as the published decisions contained in the authorised law reports, as assumptions or inferences drawn from a single source may produce misleading or inaccurate conclusions or inferences.

## Livestock Trading Account
## for the year ended 30 June 1948

| Dr | | | | Cr | | | |
|---|---|---|---|---|---|---|---|
| Date | Particulars | No. | Amount | Date | Particulars | No. | Amount |
| 1 Jul 47 | Opening stock | 110 | £1,562[248] | 14 Dec 47 | Sales | 110 | £ 550[249] |
| 14 Feb 48 | Purchases | 6 | £ 102 | 30 Jun 48 | Closing stock | 116 | £1,886 |
| 30 Jun 48 | Natural Increase | 110 | £ 110[250] | | | | |
| | Gross profit transferred to P&L A/c | | £ 662 | | | | |
| | | 226 | **£2,436** | | | 226 | **£ 2,436** |
| 1 July 48 | Opening stock | 116 | £1,886 | | | | |

Table 6: Wade's Suggested Original Livestock Trading Account.[251]

---

248 This amount was interpolated from the sums provided in the *Wade Case* (n 1) 109.

249 A fictitious figure for illustration purposes. It was assumed that if a fully grown heifer was purchased for £17, then £5 for a weaner would not be unreasonable.

250 The nearest valuation for Income Tax regulation 10(3) that could be found was in 1966. The value prescribed at that time was £1. In 1948, it may have been as little as 10/- (shillings: there were 20/- in a £); however, this figure was accepted as sufficient for illustrative purposes. Education Department of Western Australia, *Leaving Accountancy* (Technical Education Publications Trust Fund, Technical Extension Service, 1966) 415.

251 Part II.

Table 6 is a construction of Wade's livestock trading account compiled from the data provided in the decision of the *Wade Case*. The sums used reflect the assumed production of calves and the six cattle that he declared as purchases in his original income tax return.[252] The 110 cattle destroyed and then replaced do not appear in the account, in accordance with the decision.[253] This schedule shows a gross profit of £662 rather than a loss of £7. Likewise, the assessed Live Stock Schedule accompanying Wade's notice of assessment was contained in the documents found in the certified Appeal Book.[254] It is reproduced here in Table 7, shown below.

**Amended Live Stock Schedule
for the year ended 30 June 1948**

| Dr | Column A | | | | Column B | | Cr |
|---|---|---|---|---|---|---|---|
| Date | Particulars | No. | Amount | Date | Particulars | No. | Amount |
| 1 Jul 47 | Opening stock: Cattle Horses | 94 9 | £748 72 | | Sales: Cattle Horses | 134 3 | £2,224 8 |
| | Purchases: Cattle Horses | 134 6 | £2,242 75 | 30 Jun 48 | Closing stock: Cattle Horses | 114 10 | £1,383 98 |
| | Natural Increase: Cattle | 20 | | | | | |
| | | 263 | £3,137 | | | 261[255] | £3,713 |

Table 7: Amended Live Stock Schedule.

The assessment, as amended by the Commissioner, shows a net profit from livestock trading of £576, in place of the £7 loss disclosed by Wade in his income tax return. The impact of considering the

252  *Wade Case* (n 1) 106.
253  Ibid.
254  *Commissioner of Taxation v Wade* (n 201) 23.
255  The Commissioner's assessment omitted the three horses shown as deaths in Wade's income tax return.

transactions arising from the destruction of the dairy cattle and their replacement as assessable income rather than a capital transaction had the effect of increasing Wade's taxable income by £583. It is noted that, due to the nature of living animals, not only are livestock (as trading stock) costs a combination of opening stock levels and purchases the means of acquiring stock, but animals can also breed, go missing and die. Therefore those 'natural' changes in population must be valued and brought into account. The Commissioner's adjustments to bring the 'capital transactions' into the account as 'trading transactions' added the complexity of altering the closing stock value for Wade's assessable income. Therefore, instead of the closing stock of 114 cattle and 10 horses being valued at £1024, they became valued at £1481, contributing £457 to the overall increase of £583.

The Appeal Books reveal that the Taxation Board of Review found that the transaction was of a revenue nature and gave its reasons for doing so.[256] Despite Wade's argument that the dairy cattle were a capital asset, the Board decided that:

> Section 6 of the [Income Tax Assessment] Act states that, in the Act, unless the contrary intention appears, '"trading stock" includes anything produced, manufactured, acquired or purchased for the purposes of manufacture, sale or exchange and also includes live stock, and live stock does not include animals used as beasts of burden or working beasts in a business other than a business of primary production'.
> There can be no doubt that, unless the contrary intention appears, intention somewhere appears, the taxpayer's livestock i.e. his cattle, must be regarded as trading stock for the purposes of section 28. We can see nothing in section 28, or elsewhere, to suggest any contrary intention with regard to dairy cattle generally, or this taxpayer's cattle in particular. There is certainly nothing to indicate that the circumstances under which live stock has been acquired are to be enquired into for the purposes of section 28.
> 'Live stock' is 'trading stock' for the purposes of the section. If it is on hand at the beginning or end of the year of income, that is enough.[257]

Therefore, the sum of £454, being the value of Wade's cattle on hand at the end of the 1947-8 fiscal year, was considered as assessable income by the Taxation Board of Review. The Commissioner's

---

256  *Commissioner of Taxation v Wade* (n 199).
257  Ibid 52.

appeal to the High Court was as to the remainder—namely the £130, being the difference between the £2016 received as compensation, and the £1886, the cost of Wade's replacement cattle. Ultimately, that was the only matter addressed by the High Court.

> In making his assessment for that year of income the Commissioner of Taxation **added** the £2,016 to the amount shown in Wade's return under sales and the £1,866 to the amount shown under purchases, thus increasing the assessable income derived from the livestock account by the amount of £584.[258] (emphasis added)

This part argues that had the matter considered the definition of livestock as trading stock to be its central focus, the impact on the entire Live Stock Schedule as to the increased value of the closing stock would have been upheld by the court. However, as the Commissioner's action to increase the value of Wade's closing stock had been decided in the Taxation Board of Review, the residual excess of the compensation paid over the cost of replacement was the single matter addressed by the High Court. In Part II it was stated that

> the matter before the court did not consider the number of cattle or their value at the beginning of the year but rather focussed on the sum of £130 being the difference between the compensation paid (£2,016) and the expenditure of £1,886.

Therefore, this part argues that the focus of the *Wade Case* was the assessability of insurance recoveries and the deductibility of the cost of repairs relating thereto, rather than considering the concept of livestock to be trading stock, as inferred in the ATO advice. The reader is further reminded that the ATO notices contain a warning that the advice may be incorrect.[259] It may appear a little incongruous that the 'sale' and 'purchase' of livestock was considered by the Taxation Board of Review to be valid in assessing the closing value of livestock, and yet the actual trades, and profit arising, were not. Ultimately it was that single fact, the £130 profit arising from the discrepancy between the compensation monies paid to Wade and

---

258  *Wade Case* (n 1) 106.
259  Lendon (n 18).

the cost of the replacement cattle, that was considered by the High Court.

Part II noted that earlier cases focusing on the sale of livestock in Australia had found that breeding stock were not trading stock. The following section investigates why the *Wade Case* might have been appealed to the High Court if the matter had already been resolved.

## 8.5 Previous litigation presented in the *Wade Case*

Part II outlined the cases presented to the High Court in the decision of the *Wade Case*, namely:

> *Commissioners of Inland Revenue v Brooks;*[260] *Commissioners of Inland Revenue v Newcastle Breweries Ltd;*[261] *Commissioners of Inland Revenue v Northfleet Coal & Ballast Co;*[262] *Commissioners of Inland Revenue v Executors of Williams;*[263] *Danmark Pty Ltd v Federal Commissioner of Taxation;*[264] *Farnsworth v Federal Commissioner of Taxation;*[265] *The Commissioners of Inland Revenue v J Gliksten & Son, Ltd;*[266] *Maritime Electric Co Ltd v General Dairies Ltd;*[267] *The Minister for Lands v Ricketson and the Australian Mortgage, Land & Finance Co;*[268] *Short Bros., Ltd v Commissioners of Inland Revenue;*[269] *Stebbing v Metropolitan Board of Works;*[270] *Van Den Berghs, Ltd v Clark.*[271]

It found that most of the cases did not relate to the distinction between breeding stock as a capital asset and other animals held for the purposes of sale and therefore revenue assets, but rather focused on the receipt of insurance or compensation monies to be considered as assessable income. It suggests that:

---

260  (1915) AC 478.
261  (1927) 12 TC 927. Reported in K.BD, 42 TLR. 185, CA., 42 TLR. 609, and H.L, *43 TLR. 476.
262  (1927) 12 TC 1102.
263  (1943) 1 All E.R. 318.
264  (1944) 7 ATD 333.
265  [1949] HCA 27; (1949) 78 CLR 504.
266  [1929] UKHL TC 14 364 (22 February 1929).
267  (1937) AC 610.
268  (1898) 19 LR NSW 281.
269  (1927) 12 TC 955.
270  (1870) LR 6 QB 37.
271  (1935) AC 431, 19 TC 390.

> It may be that the *Wade Case* focused on insurance recoveries as assessable income and substituted monies received by way of insurance recoveries as an effective sale of livestock, instead of considering the distinction between breeding stock and trading stock.

Additionally, it also considered a number of other cases which it considered relevant to the *Wade Case* but which were not used in evidence by either party. Significantly, it examined the decision in the *Robinson Case*[272] and found that it focused on the sale of sheep in conjunction with the sale of a pastoral property. It was:

> *Held,* that the ewe weaners were not 'trading stock' within the definition of that term in sec. 4 of the *Income Tax Assessment Act* 1922-1925, and therefore that the proceeds of the sale of such ewe weaners were not assessable income of the owner under sec. 17 (1) of that Act.[273]

Part II stated that:

> The *Robinson Case* of 1927 supports the distinction but the later *Wade Case* of 1951 does not. It may be that if the *Robinson Case* had been considered by their Honours in *Wade*, then the outcome may have been different.

As the *Robinson Case* of 1927 found the opposite of the *Wade Case* of 1951 — that there is a distinction between the animals held in a business of primary production and that some are not trading stock, this research examined the amendments to the income tax legislation that occurred in the period between 1927 and 1951. It was found that s 17, referred to in the *Robinson Case*, had been repealed in 1936. Accordingly, s 17 of the *Income Tax Assessment Act* 1922-34 (*ITAA 1922*) is examined in detail in the following section of this part.

## 8.6   Section 17 — The forgotten story

This book focuses on the ATO's view that *all* livestock held in a business of primary production are trading stock, and therefore that fiscal transactions are a form of revenue according to ordinary concepts and subject to income tax. The ATO supports that view by applying the reported decision of the 1951 *Wade Case*.[274] The matter

---

272   *Robinson Case* (n 3).
273   Ibid 297.
274   Lendon (n 18).

of accounting for stud or breeding stock was previously examined in Part I and the decision of the *Wade Case* were further examined in detail in Part II.

This chapter has examined the sequence of events and documents from the lodgement of Wade's 1948 income tax return to the final appeal by the Commissioner to the Full Bench of the High Court in 1951 to investigate if the ATO's view is truly supported by the decision of the *Wade Case* or whether that opinion might be successfully challenged.

The part concludes that significant changes to taxation law have occurred over the past 70 years and that the *Wade Case* may no longer be a concrete foundation to the view that breeding or stud stock should not be treated as capital assets or aids to manufacture but rather as goods held for re-sale. This, and the preceding parts, indicate that, while the ATO opinion, which relies entirely on the *Wade Case* might be unfounded, further research, beyond the scope of this analysis, reveals that the ATO view is correct. This research found that earlier cases, such as the *Robinson Case*[275] of 1927, held that breeding or stud stock were capital assets and were therefore not subject to income tax provisions. However, in the *Wade Case* of 1951 it was understood that livestock were to be considered as trading stock. Had there been a significant a change to the legislation in the period between 1927 and 1948? The Statement of Reasons for the decision of the Board of Review[276] provides the clue. In that statement the Board refers to the consistency between the provisions of the *ITAA 1922*, and the following *Income Tax Assessment Act* (Cth) *1936* (*ITAA 1936*). In that statement the Board referred to s 50 of the 'old' act and ss 51 and 51A of the 'new' act.

However, there may have been inconsistencies. This research compared the two acts and found that section 17 is contained in the *ITAA 1922* but not in the following *ITAA 1936*. Section 17 of the *ITAA 1922* contained the following provision:

(4.) In this section— (a) the expression 'trading stock' does not include live stock which in the opinion of the Commissioner, Assistant Commissioner or

---

275  *Robinson Case* (n 3) 297.
276  *Commissioner of Taxation v Wade* (n 199) 58.

> Deputy Commissioner are ordinarily used as beasts of burden or as working beasts or for breeding purposes;[277]

Section 17 expressly identified breeding stock as NOT being trading stock. However, s 17 was deleted from the *ITAA 1936* and consequently its repeal brought *all* animals used in primary production into the livestock trading account. This part suggests, therefore, that while the basis for the view might be challenged, the ATO's view is correct. Had the assessor and the accountant known of the repeal of s 17, then the *Wade Case* would never have existed. The ATO would simply have pointed that out to the taxpayer, the Board of Review, the High Court, and so on. It appears that the repeal of s 17 became lost in history. In fairness the 1930s and 1940s were tumultuous years for Australia and the World in general. The events of the Great Depression and World War II might have overshadowed the transition of the income tax legislation from the *ITAA 1922* to the *ITAA 1936*. There were also the challenges of the First Uniform Tax Case[278] to help confuse accountants and tax administrators alike.

Detailed examination of the Ferguson Royal Commission on Taxation 1934[279] is not conducted here, but the brief relevant details as to why it recommended to repeal s 17 are outlined here. The Royal Commission considered arguments made by various graziers' associations to continue the exemption from income tax for transactions relating to the purchase and sale of breeding stock, but found that:

> The claim [by the associations that the sale of breeding stock should not be included in assessable income] is based upon the argument that live stock used for breeding purposes is equivalent to plant, and that when it is sold the proceeds should be regarded as a realization of capital. But the grazier does not take this view when he buys it, for the cost is debited to his working account, and he is allowed a deduction in full for the amount so expended. If breeding stock is sold otherwise than upon the realization of a business, the proceeds are brought to account as ordinary income, and the grazier is taxed on the profit or allowed for the loss on the transaction. If the argument

---

277  *Income Tax Assessment Act 1922* (Cth) s 17.
278  South Australia v Commonwealth ("First Uniform Tax case) [1942] HCA 14; 65 CLR 373 (23 July 1942).
279  Ferguson Royal Commission Report (n 2).

that breeding stock is capital be sound, it should be treated consistently in all circumstances, and in that event its cost would not be allowed as a deduction, nor would any profit on its realization be taxable.

The truth is that live stock possesses some of the characteristics both of a fixed asset and a trading asset. Although an animal may be acquired primarily for breeding or wool-growing purposes, its ultimate sale is in many cases by no means a minor consideration. The life of any stock is limited to a few years, and must eventually be realized or replaced.[280]

Although the argument that the assets must eventually be realized or replaced might apply to all capital assets, the dual characteristics of animals, in that they can carry out the functions of breeding stock and trading stock simultaneously is considered unique to biological assets, therefore, the Commission's rationale is difficult to refute. Accordingly, the Royal Commission made the following recommendation:

> We recommend that the proceeds of breeding stock sold upon the realization or discontinuance of a business from any cause whatever shall be included in the assessable income of the taxpayer.[281]
> We recommend that Section 17 of the Commonwealth Income Tax Assessment Act, which permits the purchaser of sheep in the wool to treat the cost as a purchase of sheep and wool as distinct from each other, be deleted from the Act.[282]

The explanatory memorandum put to parliament did not provide as much detail as that contained in the report but rather simply stated the following definition of "Live stock" does not include animals used as beasts of burden or working beasts in a business other than a business of primary production.[283] That definition reflects the repeal of s 17, which had made the distinction between breeding stock and stock held for resale. It is assumed that 'working beasts' referred to animals used to produce products for sale, that is wool, fat lambs, or milk. The following footnote was added to the explanatory memorandum to give clarification as to why the definition was to be included in the legislation:

---

280  Ferguson Report (n 4) 135.
281  Ibid.
282  Ibid 136.
283  Explanatory Memorandum, Bill for an Act to Consolidate and Amend the Income Tax Assessment Act 1922-1934, 1935 (Cth) 8.

> (e) This definition continues the existing Commonwealth practice except in regard to live stock used as working beasts and beasts of burden by primary producers. In their case, the difficulty of identifying these animals and also the necessity of accounting for any sale of the possible natural increase, make it desirable in the interests of simplicity to bring working beasts and beasts of burden into the live stock schedule.[284]

It is noted that the reason provided for the removal of s 17 in the Royal Commission report—that is, the inability to treat the value of a sheep (a capital asset) in distinction from its wool (a revenue asset)—was not contained in the explanatory memorandum. Section 17 was duly omitted from the *ITAA 1936*, and therefore *all* animals used in a business of primary production became classified as trading stock regardless of the function those animals carry out. It is that basis that the ATO should place its support for its view and not the decision of the *Wade Case* which, as discussed, might be challenged.

Discussion of how breeding stock could be accounted for, other than by being included in the general category of livestock, is beyond the scope of this book. However, Allen has considered the concept in detail and concludes that:

> The tax community should be aware of how the present system for taxing live stock came about and, in particular, why the current valuation methods were avoided for so many years. When the current system fails, a better one will be needed based on sound logic and analysis.[285]

It might also be noted that an aging merino ewe, used for growing wool and producing merino lambs for wool production, might be sent to the abattoir at the end of her 'useful life' but to consider her and a dorper fat lamb bred specifically for the prime lamb meat market to be synonymous might reveal a simplistic view of the pastoral industry. That discussion might be considered in future research.

---

284   Ibid 9.
285   Christina Allen, 'Taxation of Live Stock in Australia: A Critical Review of Tax Law and Policy' (2020) 49(3) *Australian Law Review* 209, 231.

## 8.7 Summary and Conclusion

This part argues that rulings and determinations issued by the ATO should not be considered by tax practitioners as always providing greater clarity and certainty in the preparation and lodgement of taxation returns and the payment of tax. It notes that tax agents are duty bound by law to take reasonable care to ensure that taxation laws are applied correctly to the circumstances in relation to which they are providing advice to a client[286] and accordingly it asserts that agents should not simply accept that the ATO view on a matter as necessarily representing the correct view of an issue. Significantly, it notes that the ATO is not directly responsible for the mistaken belief that rulings and advice given by it provides irrefutable grounds for a particular view or interpretation of tax law. While the ATO may provide guidance on its view, those opinions clearly include a caveat that its opinion may be not be correct. Its written opinions generally include a specific disclaimer which states:

> If this advice turns out to be incorrect and you underpay your tax as a result, you will not have to pay a penalty. Nor will you have to pay interest on the underpayment provided you reasonably relied on the advice in good faith. However, even if you don't have to pay a penalty or interest, you will have to pay the correct amount of tax.[287]

To illustrate this argument, the part uses the case of livestock held in a business of primary production. In Parts I and II, the authors argued that animals kept for stud or breeding purposes should be considered capital assets and that the proceeds of sale of those assets should be subject to capital gains tax provisions and concessions. However, they found that the ATO considered *all* animals held in a business of primary production to be held for the purpose of sale and the proceeds of sale to be subject to income tax regardless of their primary function.

   On investigation it was found that the word *all* was not contained in the legislation but rather that the ATO relied on the decision of the *Wade Case* to support its view. The authors found that that view had remained unchallenged for over 70 years when they

---

286  Code of Professional Conduct (n 191).
287  Lendon (n 18).

conducted their subsequent investigation of the *Wade Case*. This investigation focused on the reported decision of the *Wade Case* which revealed that their Honours had used the inference that *all* livestock were trading stock to reach their decisions. It was discovered that the decision of the *Wade Case* was not as conclusive as the ATO view suggested, and that in particular, Kitto J was reluctant to accept that principle, but he focused instead on the concept of insurance recoveries and the costs of repairs to support his decision.[288]

Therefore, based solely on the reported decision of the *Wade Case*, it was found that sufficient doubt existed to suggest the Commissioner's view might not be reliably supported by the decision of the *Wade Case*. Rather they supported the argument that some animals held in a business of primary production, such as horses and dogs used for mustering and stud stock used for breeding, or the production of animal products, such as milk or wool, are of a capital nature and should be treated accordingly for taxation purposes.

However, the arguments in Parts I and II did not reveal the background to the *Wade Case* which may have consolidated or refuted the ATO view and this left the matter open for further research. The subsequent research supporting this part reveals why it was *inferred* that *all* animals held in a business of primary production are considered trading stock. It is not the decision the *Wade Case*, as suggested by the ATO advice, but rather the operation of the Law.

In 1934, the section of the *ITAA 1922-34* that segregated breeding stock from livestock held for trading purposes was repealed.[289] This part reveals that the impact of that change in the legislation brought Wade's dairy cattle into his livestock schedule as assessed by the Commissioner of Taxation. This research reveals that Wade appealed first to the CTBR and then to a single judge of the High Court (Kitto J). His appeal was based on the distinction between animals held for production purposes and therefore should be considered as capital assets, but while the distinction of his dairy cattle being a means of production — a capital asset, and not a product for sale — a revenue asset, s 17 was not considered in any evidence provided to the CTRB or the High Court. Section 17 expressly

---

288 Ibid.
289 *Income Tax Assessment Act 1922* s 17.

identified that breeding stock were NOT trading stock. However, s 17 was omitted from the *ITAA 1936*, and consequently its omission brought *all* animals used in primary production into the livestock trading account. Therefore, this part suggests that while the basis for the view might be challenged, the ATO view is correct.

The conclusion of this part is that had the assessor and the accountant known of the repeal of s 17, the *Wade Case* would never have existed. The ATO could simply have pointed that out to the taxpayer, the Board of Review, the High Court and so on. It also acknowledges that to research every matter of precedent reported and used in the courts to the level conducted in this research would be an unrealistic expectation for tax preparers, legal practitioners and the courts to conduct it does highlight the need to carry out independent research the background of similar cases. This part points to the statutory requirement that tax agents are duty bound to take reasonable care to ensure that taxation laws are applied correctly to the circumstances in relation to which they are providing advice to a client[290] and in that context, it asserts that agents should not simply accept the ATO view on a matter as necessarily representing the correct view of an issue.

The final part of this book highlights the fiscal dangers of accepting ATO opinions without challenge and recommends that tax practitioners should conduct their own legislative research and make their own interpretations of statutes. If the decision of the *Wade Case* forms a problematic basis for a particular view, and the ATO cannot be held liable, there may well be other rulings and opinions equally as challengeable.

---

290  Code of Professional Conduct (n 191) s 30-10.

# PART IV

# AUSTRALIAN TAXATION OFFICE PRONOUNCEMENTS: WHY TAX ADVISERS NEED TO EXERCISE CAUTION

*This part was first published as an article in the Journal of Australian Taxation in December 2022 24(1). It is re-published here mutatis mutandis with permission of the publisher.*

*This part warns that tax practitioners should not always consider that the rulings, determinations and advice provided by the ATO give the greater clarity and certainty in the preparation and lodgement of taxation returns and the payment of tax that are sought by practitioners.*

# Chapter Nine
# The Trap

## 9.1 Introduction

In the modern environment of complex taxation law there is ever-evolving legislation and interpretation. To maintain the high professional standards that are ethically and legally required, tax practitioners are obliged to engage in close scrutiny of the law to obtain a clear understanding. However, tax practitioners find it increasingly difficult to keep themselves informed while dealing with the pressures of their workloads. Therefore, to assist practitioners, professional bodies are constantly providing information and commentary about changes to statutory and case law. Further, the ATO issues its own interpretations, rulings and other such proclamations, to guide taxpayers and practitioners and assist in compliance.

The authors' research suggests that the sometimes confusing and apparently convoluted legislative change and evolving case law are leading practitioners to become increasingly reliant on ATO rulings and advice rather than conducting their own legislative research and making their own interpretations of statutes. This part argues that the practice of accepting ATO opinions without challenge can have extremely significant fiscal impacts on taxpayers and tax collections. It warns that tax practitioners should not always consider that the rulings, determinations and advice provided by the ATO give the greater clarity and certainty in the preparation and lodgement of taxation returns and the payment of tax that are sought by practitioners.

Tax agents are duty bound to take reasonable care to ensure that taxation laws are applied correctly to the circumstances in relation to which they are providing advice to a client,[291] and in that context this book asserts that agents should not accept that the ATO's view on a matter is unquestionably correct. Further, it is noted that, while the ATO provides guidance and views, their

---

291  Code of Professional Conduct (n 191) s 30-10.

written advice usually contains a statement to the effect that they are for guidance only and may not be binding in a court. Their written opinions often include a specific disclaimer that states:

> If this advice turns out to be incorrect and you underpay your tax as a result, you will not have to pay a penalty. Nor will you have to pay interest on the underpayment provided you reasonably relied on the advice in good faith. However, even if you don't have to pay a penalty or interest, you will have to pay the correct amount of tax.[292]

Therefore, it is clear that the ATO assumes no responsibility to taxpayers or practitioners for misinterpretations or misapplications of the law. Taxpayers and their agents must make reasonable independent inquiry to ensure compliance and the correct payment of tax.

## 9.2 Liability for Giving Advice

This book examines an uncommon, but significant, business transaction that occurs in rural and remote Australia each year—the sale of a pastoral lease by a sole trader, partnership, or similar business structure. In the sale of a pastoral and farming property as a going concern, the ATO view is that *all* animals held in a business of primary production are considered to be trading stock, regardless of the function that they perform in that business. The impact of this is that all receipts from the sale of animals in conjunction with the sale of a primary production business are taxed as income according to ordinary concepts. Therefore, individual pastoralists, graziers and farmers are denied the tax concessions that other business proprietors are granted on the sale of capital assets included in the transfer of their businesses.

In Part I, the authors challenge that opinion and argue that animals used for breeding or other purposes are not trading stock, but rather should be considered as capital assets used for the purposes of manufacture. They argue that the word *all* is not contained in s 995 of the *Income Tax Assessment Act 1997* (*ITAA 1997*), and they note that the ATO relies on the decision in the *Wade Case* to validate

---

292  Lendon (n 18).

its opinion. They find that the ATO's reliance on the decision in the *Wade Case* for support may be somewhat problematic.

They argue that there *is* a distinction between breeding animals and livestock produced for sale, and that such animals should be accounted for and taxed accordingly. They' research has established that, while the ATO view is correct, it is based on a false premise and might fail if challenged in court. However, it appears that tax professionals have generally accepted the ATO view without challenge for over 70 years, and have been advising their clients accordingly. It is their view that, if the matter were to be challenged and taxpayers were found to have been overpaying tax, then the caveat contained in the ATO advice might place the liability on the professionals providing the advice to the taxpayer and not on the ATO.

## 9.3 The *Wade Case* Study

In Part III the authors have examined the evidence presented to the High Court in the *Wade Case* to consolidate their argument. The preceding parts look at the ATO advice that *all* animals held in a business of primary production are trading stock, and the basis on which the ATO holds that belief. Part III turns to the events leading to the *Wade Case* and investigates previous similar cases as well as amendments to Australia's income tax assessment acts and find that, while the ATO advice is correct, the basis for that view is not.

It is the ATO's view is that it:

> considers that the definition of live stock in section 995-1 of the *Income Tax Assessment Act 1997* includes all animals in a primary production business for the reason that the majority ruling of Dixon and Fullagar JJ in the High Court Decision of *Federal Commissioner of Taxation v Wade* (1951) 84 CLR 105 (*Wade's Case*) provides [that] 'The definition of trading stock brings "live stock" within s 36(1). There is a definition of livestock which, by inference, makes it clear that all animals are to be included case of a business of primary production. Notwithstanding, therefore, the taxpayer's claim that the destruction and replacement of 110 head of his dairy herd is a capital

transaction it is clear enough that for the purposes of s 36(1) the cattle fall within the expression of "trading stock".[293]

Despite the fact that, intuitively, stud bulls, cows, rams and ewes as well as dairy cattle, mustering horses and dogs might be considered, and valued, as aids to manufacture rather than as trading stock held for the purposes of sale, the matter appears to have been unchallenged for over 70 years. It appears that retiring pastoralists, graziers and farmers have remitted income tax on the basis that the proceeds of the sale of their stock in conjunction with the sale of their properties is income according to ordinary concepts, or a trading profit rather than a capital gain. Consequently, the authors argue, these taxpayers have over-remitted tax on the basis of advice provided by their tax advisers, accountants and other professionals.

The authors investigated the reported decision in the *Wade Case* and concluded that:

> Based solely on the reported decision of the *Wade Case*, [the authors] found that sufficient doubt existed to suggest the Commissioner's view might not be reliably supported by the decision of the *Wade Case*. Instead, the reported decision supported the argument that some animals held in a business of primary production, such as horses and dogs used for mustering, stud stock used for breeding, or animals used for the production of animal products, such as milk or wool, are of a capital nature and should be treated accordingly for taxation purposes.[294]

Subsequently, the authors' research looked beyond the reported decision of the *Wade Case* and found that hearings before the Commonwealth Taxation Board of Review and an earlier case heard by the High Court provide evidence and background that is not presented in the authorised case reports.[295] They suggest that the reasons given by Dixon and Fullagar JJ for their decision may have been taken out of context by the ATO. They note that:

> Dixon and Fullagar JJ accepted the concept that the cattle were to be considered trading stock, and therefore of a revenue nature, irrespective of the role

---

293  Lendon (n 18).
294  Reproduced from Part III For reader convenience.
295  *Wade v Commissioner of Taxation*, Commonwealth Taxation Board of Review No. 2. (1950) No M37/1950. Note: The matter is also reported as (1950) 1 CTBR (NS) Case 77, 335; and (1950) 1TBRD Case 72, 273: and in Gunn and O'Neill (n 201).

that they played in the business. They also noted that Kitto J was reluctant to accept that principle, but focused instead on the concept of insurance recoveries and the costs of repairs to support his decision.

Fullarton and Pinto also pointed to a number of relevant previous cases that were not considered by the High Court. Without supporting documentation other than the report published in the *Commonwealth Law Reports* it could not be concluded whether their Honours were aware of those cases, or whether they had been omitted from either the evidence or the reported decisions.[296]

Therefore, the authors argue that, while the ATO considers that the main decision of the High Court was focused on animals held in a business of primary production, and from this infers that *all* animals are held as trading stock regardless of their role in that business, the *Wade Case* was focused on the assessment of monies paid to a taxpayer in compensation for a loss. Wade had been compensated for the loss and replacement of his assets, and that is the primary matter addressed by the court. That those assets happened to be dairy cows and not a milking shed or some other assets is not specifically relevant to the decision, but what was relevant was the assessment of the surplus funds of £130 left over from the compensation received by Wade and the cost of purchasing the replacement cows. The authors argue that the judges' comments as to the classification of the lost assets (dairy cows) are *obiter dictum* rather than central to the matter decided, and might not be regarded as legal precedent in subsequent cases.

The authors found that a 1927 case considered by the High Court concerning the classification of livestock had held that ewe weaners were not trading stock as they were held for the purposes of breeding, and that the proceeds of the sale of such ewe weaners were not assessable income.[297] That decision is in direct conflict with the *inference* that *all* animals held in a business of primary production are trading stock and not capital assets. Therefore, a further investigation was conducted into why the 1927 decision in the *Robinson Case* was different to the judges' supporting statements in the *Wade Case* of 1951.

---

296  Reproduced from Part III For reader convenience.
297  *Robinson Case* (n 3).

It was found that s 17 of the *Income Tax Assessment Act 1922*, in force until 1936, expressly excluded livestock which, in the opinion of the Commissioner, Assistant Commissioner or Deputy Commissioner, were ordinarily used as beasts of burden or as working beasts or for breeding purposes. However, s 17 had been deliberately repealed, to bring all animals into the Live Stock Trading Schedule for assessment for income tax, on the recommendation of the Royal Commission on Taxation 1932-34.[298] Therefore, it is the repeal of that legislation which renders *all* animals held in a business of primary production trading stock, not the decision of the *Wade Case*. The ATO view may be correct, but it is based on the wrong reasons.

The authors point to that flaw in the ATO's published view to draw the attention of tax professionals and academics to the need to conduct diligent research in giving advice to taxpayers. In this case, it might be said that the ATO 'got lucky', but the advice clearly contains the caveat that it is not to be relied on, other than to indemnify taxpayers from penalties and interest if the advice is incorrect, and therefore the responsibility lies entirely on the giver of the advice and not the ATO. The authors further suggest that if this particular advice might be successfully challenged — the matter decided was the assessment of insurance recoveries and not the classification of animals — then, given the number of rulings, opinions and determinations issued by the ATO, there are almost certainly others that would fail under intense scrutiny and challenge. This highlights that a failure to carry out reasonable investigations may result in false beliefs and cause considerable fiscal damage to taxpayers. Failure to take note of the ATO's caveat could leave tax professionals liable to claims of negligence.

---

298  Ferguson Report (4) 135.

# Chapter Ten
# Final Observations, Summary and Conclusions

## 10.1   Final Observations

The authors make the following observations as to the conduct and findings of their research:

1.  The definition of livestock as trading stock, and therefore as products for sale rather than capital assets used as aids to manufacture, is a matter of legislation not case law. It is the operation and repeal of s 17 which determines the classification, not the decision in the *Wade Case*. If a challenge to the ATO view was to be determined on the evidence of the report in the *Wade Case*, reasonable evidence would need to be submitted to the court (such as accurate accounting and animal breeding records) to show that trading livestock were segregated from breeding livestock, and it would be argued that the *Wade Case* primarily considered the assessment of insurance and compensation monies as ordinary income. Taxpayers might then successfully argue that the proceeds of the sale of their breeding stock should be taxed according to the capital gains tax provisions and not as income according to ordinary concepts.

    Section 17 was repealed on the recommendation of the Ferguson Royal Commission, but the reason given by the Royal Commission was not the same as that given to Parliament for the repeal. The Royal Commission report points to the difficulty in separating a sheep (a capital asset) from its wool (a revenue asset). The explanatory memorandum accompanying the Bill recommended the repeal of s 17 as a matter of simplicity.

    Parliamentarians might instead have amended the Bill to add a sub-section to ensure that sheep were sold 'off-shears' (that is, s 17 would apply to shorn sheep but not to those 'in wool'). Taxpayers might then have been able to classify their animals as plant, providing they were shorn. That amendment would have addressed the Royal Commission's concern without removing s 17 entirely.

The *Income Tax Assessment Act 1997* could be amended to clarify the matter addressed by the authors, and the argument that breeding stock should be considered as plant rather than as goods for sale could be settled.

The findings of this research validate the current ATO view, but do not settle the core argument that retiring pastoralists, farmers and graziers are being deprived of capital gains tax concessions, to which other business proprietors are entitled, on the disposal of their businesses.

2.  The interest in this point of tax law shown by the accounting profession has been rather low. Despite several approaches to members of the Institute of Public Accountants generally and individual approaches to rural and urban tax agents, only 110 respondents were willing to participate in this research. The matter was generally of little or no interest to urban practices, few of which have clients who might be impacted by the ATO view.

    The number of taxpayers in Western Australia engaged in disposing of pastoral properties averaged just ten per year over the past 20 years. No investigation was made as to farmers' views. The lack of volume of transactions might explain the general lack of awareness of and interest in this issue by taxation practitioners.

3.  A key observation goes to the root of this research — had
    Wade's accountant been aware of the repeal of s 17 then he
    might have disclosed the disposal and purchase of replace-
    ment dairy cows in Wade's 1948 income tax return, instead of
    appending a note disclosing the transactions. Had the as-
    sessing clerk been aware of the repeal of s 17 then he might
    have advised Wade at the point of amendment and the rea-
    son. Had the Crown solicitor been aware of the repeal of s 17
    then the fact might have been presented to the Common-
    wealth Taxation Review Board and Wade's appeal would
    have been dismissed.

Had Kitto J been advised of the repeal of s 17 then he may
not have had:

> some difficulty in accepting the view that the fact that dairy cattle, which are
> not trading stock according to ordinary concepts, are required [to be] by force
> of a definition to be taken into account under ss 28 and 32 of the *Income Tax
> Assessment Act* 1936-1947 (Cth) as trading stock.[299]

There are many historical reasons, not least the social and
economic upheavals of The Great Depression and World War
Two in the years between 1934 and 1948, which may have
caused the repeal of s 17 and the impact on the application of
income tax on primary producers. However, the key lesson
from this research is that reliance on memory, or the opinions
of others not qualified to conduct legal research and provide
legal advice as to legislation, can lead to very expensive outcomes for the courts, administrators and taxpayers.

Perhaps all of those involved relied on what had been the
legislation the last time they had had to address the matter —
just after the Great Depression, and 'before the war'. Times and
the legislation had changed but they did not know that. The
authors suggest that it is hard to judge whether they ought to
have known in 1951, but in 2023, those professionals and academics engaged in providing taxation law advice for remuner-
ation are ethically and legally bound to ensure they have a

---

299  *Wade Case* (n1) 114.

sound knowledge of the legislation, and they should not rely on the opinions or views of others. That caveat certainly applies to advice or opinions given by the ATO, which points to doubt in relying on such advice or opinions.

4.  The authors also note the opinion of Mc Nab, who casts doubt on the value of private rulings as in a number of cases the Courts have failed to give effect to them. He suggests that events occurring after the ruling is issued, such as changes in corporate structure or legislation, can render the ruling superfluous. He further suggests that sometimes the cost of applying for a private ruling can outweigh the benefits to the taxpayer relying on the ruling.

    However, he also points to

    The key benefit of such a ruling is found in s 357-60 [ITAA 1997] which states that "a ruling" "binds the Commissioner" in relation to "you". If it applies to you, and you rely on it by acting (or omitting to act) in accordance with it, the Commissioner is then unable to increase your tax liability in relation to the subject-matter of the ruling, or apply penalties and interest if there is a later disagreement. This certainty can be valuable.[300]

## 10.2   Summary and Conclusions

This book has challenged the view held by the ATO and nearly half of the accountants and tax preparers in Australia that ALL animals in a primary production business are considered livestock for the purposes of the trading stock provisions of the ITAA 1997. The impact of that view is that retiring pastoralists and farmers are levied income tax at ordinary rates on the proportion of animals held for breeding or stud purposes as part of the business.

The view held by the ATO denies retiring pastoralists and farmers certain exemptions and concessions permitted under the CGT provisions. It obliges them to pay the higher personal income tax rates assessed on income according to ordinary concepts, rather than permit them access to the tax concessions that should be

---

300  Paul Mc Nab 'Private Rulings: Are they worth it?' (2022) 57(1) *Taxation in Australia* 38,39.

afforded to them on the disposal of their properties and their subsequent retirement.

This chapter affirms the argument stated on page 46 which, for reader convenience, is repeated here in full.

> that those animals kept for breeding purposes are capital assets, and therefore the proceeds of the sale of those animals, in conjunction with the sale of the property and other assets contained thereon for the purpose of operating the business, are capital sales. Thus, that proportion of the proceeds of the sale of the primary production business should be subject to CGT provisions and taxed accordingly.

This part examined the findings of the *Wade Case* and argues that the findings of it may be somewhat misunderstood by the ATO in support of its firm view. The decision was indeed based on the view that ALL animals in a primary production business are livestock for trading purposes, but it focussed on the replacement of dairy cattle destroyed for disease-control purposes. Other working animals, such as horses and dogs used for mustering and control of stock, were not considered.

Therefore, the presumption that ALL animals are not capital assets may not be as reliable as it appears. In order for the ATO view to be entirely supported, it must apply to ALL animals absolutely. Once exceptions are established, then the precedent may not be as absolute as it is currently considered by the ATO.

In addition, Kitto J, dissenting, considered s 26(j), and related ITAA 1936 provisions. He noted the net proceeds of insurance recoveries rather than the profit generated from transactions in the livestock trading account. He also stated that he had difficulty in accepting the concept that dairy cattle were trading stock. Nonetheless, he made the assumption that the dairy cattle were trading stock in order to apply his findings under s 26(j).

This book considers that the findings of the *Robinson Case* are so similar to the case study considered here that considerable doubt can be placed on the ATO's opinion that ALL livestock in a business of primary production are trading stock according to ordinary concepts. Animals kept for the purposes of breeding should be regarded as capital assets and subject to capital gains tax and accompanying concessions upon their disposal.

It is noted that the *Wade Case* of 1951 relies substantially on British cases for precedent. In 1951, the British courts were courts of appeal for Australian cases. British court findings have not bound Australian courts since 1986;[301] therefore, the precedents set by those cases, which bound the High Court in 1951, no longer apply. It is argued that if the *Wade Case* were held in modern times, the outcome may be somewhat different. Further, since the *Wade Case* of 1951, capital gains tax has been introduced (1985) and the Asprey Report of 1975 indicated that livestock could be considered capital assets rather than trading stock. In addition, the introduction of accounting standards relating to biological assets since 2000 indicate that the ATO view may not be as relevant in 2020 as it was before those events.

This book concludes that despite the complexities of recording the transactions for accounting purposes and for taxation lodgement compliance, the matter of the distinction between animals held long-term for their produce rather than held in the short term for trading purposes should be reconsidered by the ATO, stakeholders and the accounting/tax professions. The associated accounting standards are beyond the scope of this book. However, it is suggested that the adoption of AASB 141 will ultimately make that review essential.

A detailed examination of tax accounting processes for dealing with the recording and reporting of financial statements pertaining to livestock was conducted in the Part I 'Tax Accounting for Livestock: Mother or Meat/Capital or Revenue'. That part examines the distinction between classifying expenditures by an enterprise as capital (assets purchased) or revenue (costs of operation).

Part III finds that the consideration that *all* animals held in a business of primary production in Australia are classified as trading stock is a matter of taxation legislation. That was not always the case. Prior to its repeal in 1934, s 17 of the *ITAA 1922-34* provided that breeding stock were considered capital assets. The basis of

---

301 *Australia Act* 1986 (Cth).

Wade's omission of the transactions relating to the destruction and replacement of his dairy cattle was that it was argued that the cattle were not trading stock but, rather were aids to manufacture and therefore 'purely a capital transaction', as noted in his 1948 income tax return.

It argues that breeding stock should be treated as capital assets. It points to the effluxion of time, the recommendations of the Asprey Report[302] and the introduction of capital gains tax in 1985 as factors which should lead to the reclassification of some livestock as capital assets rather than trading stock, regardless of their function in the business. The 1934 Ferguson Royal Commission on Taxation recommended the repeal of s 17 of the *ITAA 1922-34* to simplify the distinction between livestock as capital assets and their products as revenue assets. However, the basis for the recommendation was not the difficulty in distinguishing stud sheep from market sheep but, rather, the difficulty in distinguishing a sheep from its wool.[303] That detail was omitted from the explanatory memorandum given with the Bill to enact the *ITAA 1936*.

Therefore, while it is accepted that *all* animals held in a business of primary production are considered to be trading stock by operation of the legislation, the matter as to why breeding stock, and other animals held as aids to manufacture should not be regarded as capital assets remains. It is inequitable that retiring farmers, pastoralists and graziers should pay significantly more tax on the proceeds of the sale of their businesses than do other business owners do on the sale of their capital assets due to their breeding or stud animals being regarded as trading stock by operation of the law. This book suggests that the repeal of s 17 should be investigated and researched such that the situation argued by Wade, and addressed by statute prior to 1934, be reinstated and accounted for using modern electronic data processing systems and accounting procedures to permit the distinctions to be effectively returned to farmers, pastoralists and graziers for taxation purposes. What may

---

302  Asprey report (n 43).
303  Ferguson Royal Commission Report (n 2) 135.

have been complex in 1934 may be simpler in the twenty-first century.

Therefore, notwithstanding the discussions put in this book, it is suggested that if the proper accounting and stock identification and recording systems are held, then despite the repeal of s 17, stud or breeding stock can be considered capital assets. The proceeds of sale of those animals would then be subject to CGT rather than income tax and therefore eligible for the appropriate CGT concessions.

Finally, Part IV points to a flaw in the ATO's published view that *all* livestock held in a business of primary production are revenue rather than capital assets and draws the attention of tax professionals and academics to the need to conduct diligent research in giving advice to taxpayers. It suggests that in the case examined in this book that it might be said that the ATO 'got lucky'. It also warns that ATO advice usually contains a clear the caveat that it is not to be relied on as formal legal advice but rather only acts to indemnify taxpayers from penalties and interest if the advice is incorrect and the taxpayer proves the advice was relied upon in good faith. Therefore, liability for any loss or damage arising from the use of that advice lies entirely on the giver of the advice and not the ATO.

# Chapter Eleven
# Suggestions for Further Research

Part III noted that the existence of two authorised court reporting publications: the Australasian Tax Decisions[304] and the Commonwealth Law Report.

An example was given that the preamble presented in Australasian Tax Decisions version report of the *Wade Case* contains a detailed reproduction of the Commissioner's calculations to the adjustments of the Live Stock Schedule however the Commonwealth Law Report version does not. The Commonwealth Law Report version contains the same detail, but in word form rather than set out in an accounting form. Detailed discussion of the impacts of the existence of two publications is beyond the scope of this book but might be considered in future research.

This has found that reliance on ATO publications on its interpretation of tax law may be helpful to tax professionals but it should not be relied on as conclusive argument. Most ATO publications contain a caveat as to the limitations of using its publications as support for legal support. Therefore, taxpayers and tax professionals should seek independent legal advice when preparing tax returns.

This book has found one example of where changes in legislation and accounting practices have resulted in litigation which might have been avoided if the parties involved had known of the changes in the Law in 1948. This book has established that subsequent ATO opinions on the matter investigated are correct, but incorrectly supported. The opinion, based on a 1951 case, might be challenged more than 70 years later. It is suggested that other mistakes or misinterpretation of ATO opinions and guidelines might exist. Given the many hundreds of ATO publications currently in

---

304 The *Australian Tax Decisions* (ATD) series contains Australian tax cases from 1930 to 1969. The ATD series was originally published in 15 volumes by the Law Book Company. It was sometimes known as Australasian Tax Decisions.

existence it is almost certain that other examples are being relied on and should be investigated for validity.

Part III looked at the brief relevant details as to why the Ferguson Royal Commission on Taxation 1934[305] recommended to repeal s 17 are outlined here but it was not examined in detail. Despite the Royal Commission report being nearly 100 years old this research has found that its recommendations play a significant role in the interpretation and application in the modern world. This book suggests the report of the Ferguson Royal Commission of 1934 might be further investigated and compared with the amendments adopted in the ITAA 1936 and the later ITAA 1997 to establish if any other 'anomalies' might exist.

Further, as to how breeding stock could be accounted for, other than by being included in the general category of livestock, was not conducted in this research, however other researchers such as Allen have considered the concept in more detail. Given changes to international standards for accounting for biological assets, it is recommended that future research could investigate and focus on that concept.

---

305  Ferguson Royal Commission Report (n 2).

# APPENDIX 'A'

## ATO Guidance Letter, Lendon to Fullarton
## 6 November 2019

GPO Box 9990 IN YOUR CAPITAL CITY AUSTRALIA

**Australian Government**
**Australian Taxation Office**

Dr Alexander Fullarton
PO Box 180
CARNARVON QA 6701

| | |
|---|---|
| Reply to: | PO Box 3575 |
| | ALBURY NSW 2640 |
| Our reference: | 1051520279706 |
| Contact officer: | Matthew Busby |
| Phone: | 07 4753 7965 |

6 November 2019

**Taxation advice - For your information**

Dear Dr Fullarton

**Subject: Live stock in a primary production business**
In response to your request for advice dated 9 April 2019, we offer the following advice.

**Questions you have asked:**
You asked us whether all animals in a primary production business are considered live stock for the purposes of the trading stock provisions.

**Answers to your questions:**
The Commissioner considers that the definition of live stock in section 995-1 of the *Income Tax Assessment Act 1997* includes all animals in a primary production business for the following reasons:

The majority ruling of Dixon and Fullager JJ in the High Court decision of *Federal Commissioner of Taxation v Wade* (1951) 84 CLR 105 (*Wade's* case) provides at paragraphs 6 and 7:

> In support of his appeal against this decision the commissioner relied primarily on s. 36 (1) and (8) (a). Section 36 (1) provides that "where the whole or any part of the assets of a business carried on by a taxpayer is disposed of by sale or otherwise howsoever, whether for the purpose of putting an end to the business or any part thereof or not, and the assets disposed of include any property being trading stock... the value of that property shall be included in his assessable income, and any person acquiring that property shall be deemed to have purchased it at the amount of that value." Sub-section (8) (a) provides that, for the purposes of the section, "(a) the value of any property or live stock shall be - (i) the market value of the property or live stock on the day of the disposal; or (ii) if, in the opinion of the Commissioner, there is insufficient evidence of the market value on that day - the value which in his opinion is fair and reasonable." (at p110)

> The definition of "trading stock", as has already been mentioned, brings "live stock" within s. 36 (1). There is a definition of livestock which, by inference, makes it clear that all animals are to be included in the case of a business of primary production. Notwithstanding, therefore, the taxpayer's claim that the destruction and replacement of 110 head of his dairy herd is a capital transaction, it is clear enough that for the purposes of s. 36 (1) the cattle fall within the expression "trading stock". (at p110)

And further at paragraph 15:

> In the present case the only difficulty in the application of the principle illustrated by these passages is that a dairy herd does not consist of animals in which the dairy farmer trafficks. The taxpayer's primary source of income was the production of milk. His return for the purposes of income tax in this case shows that his substantial income is set down as the sale of milk, cream, butter and cheese. The amount shown as obtained from the sale of his dairy cattle is comparatively insubstantial. The Federal Act, however, places all animals in the category of trading stock in the case of taxpayers carrying on a business. It requires the animals on hand at the beginning and end of the period to be taken into account and inferentially the purchase and sale of such animals. Does it not follow that, apart altogether from the operation of specific provisions such as s. 36 (1) and s. 26 (j), sums of money which are received in respect of such animals should also be brought into account? The principle which the commissioner invokes relates to receipts which represent or replace stock the value of which must be taken into the trading account forming the

*basis of the ascertainment of taxable income. Whether assets of a given description form stock which must be taken into that account depends on other principles or rules the application of which is determined by the income tax law. The Income Tax Assessment Act 1936-1947 specifically provides, by means of s. 28 and the definitions in s. 6 (1) of "trading stock" and "live stock", that animals such as those destroyed shall be taken into account as stock for the purpose of the ascertainment of taxable income. By so providing the Act brings them under the operation of the principle which requires that a receipt representing an asset brought into the income account must be treated as income. It is not a sufficient answer to say that when s. 28 and the definitions in s. 6 (1) place a dairy herd in the position of stock in trade their operation is artificial. What should be treated as stock in trade is for the legislature to determine. As it has decided that such animals must be taken into account as trading stock, it follows that the compensation representing them must be treated as an item on account of revenue for the purpose of ascertaining the taxable income. (at p114)*

The definition under section 6(1) ITAA 1936 was:

**live stock** does not include animals used as beasts of burden or working beasts in a business other than a business of primary production.

The definition under section 995-1ITAA 1997 is:

**live stock** does not include animals used as beasts of burden or working beasts in a business other than a primary production business.

Whilst *Wade's* case deals with the former sections under the 1936 Act, the principles remain relevant to the current definition of live stock. Where a primary production business is carried on, then the animals used in it (for whatever purpose) will meet the definition.

ATO Interpretative Decision 2003/726: *Income Tax Definition of live stock and animal embryos* (ATO ID 2003/726) provides the Commissioner's view that the definition of live stock does not include embryos. The view is consistent with *Wade's* case where any animal used in a primary production business is trading stock under paragraph 70-10(1)(b) ITAA 1997, by virtue of the definition in section 995-1 ITAA 1997. The view distinguishes embryos from being live stock, as they are not yet animals.

This approach is applied consistently in Taxation Ruling 2008/2: *Income tax: various income tax issues relating to the horse industry; including whether racing, training and breeding activities (carried out as stand-alone activities or in combination) amount to the carrying on of a business* (TR 2008/2). The Commissioner's view consistently applies the ruling from *Wade's* case in the example tables provided in paragraphs 18, 25 and 34. In these examples, it depends on the business carried on (primary or non-primary production) and whether the assets are trading stock or depreciating assets.

In your submissions, you correctly point out that the word *all* is not contained in the section 995-1 ITAA 1997 definition. However, as per Wade's case above, the High Court ruled that all animals in a primary production business were captured under definition of livestock. This is because it is an exclusive, rather than inclusive definition.

**Relevant taxation provisions:**
*Income Tax Assessment Act* section 70-10
*Income Tax Assessment Act* section 70-90
*Income Tax Assessment Act* section 995-1

**This advice provides you with the following level of protection:**
**Interest and penalty protection**
If this advice turns out to be incorrect and you underpay your tax as a result, you will not have to pay a penalty. Nor will you have to pay interest on the underpayment provided you reasonably relied on the advice in good faith. However, even if you don't have to pay a penalty or interest, you will have to pay the correct amount of tax.

**For more information**
If you have any questions, please phone **13 28 69** between 8.00am and 5.00pm, Monday to Friday, and ask for Matthew Busby on extension **37965**, or call direct on **07 4753 7965**.

Yours sincerely


Alison Lendon
Deputy Commissioner of Taxation

Per
(Matthew Busby)

# BIBLIOGRAPHY

## A Articles/Books/Reports

Allen, Christina, 'Taxation of Live Stock in Australia: A critical review of Tax Law and Policy' (2020) 49(3) *Australian Law Review* 209

Michael Bazley et al, Contemporary Accounting: *A Conceptual Approach* (3rd ed, Nelson Australia, 1999) 49; see also Garry Carnegie et al, *Financial Accounting: Financial and Organisational Decision Making* (McGraw-Hill,1999)

Cook, Catriona, et al. *Laying Down the Law* (Butterworths 5th ed, 2001) 82

Corbin, Juliet, and Anselm Strauss *Basics of Qualitative Research* (3rd ed, Sage, 2008)

Cresswell, John Ward, *Research Design: Qualitative, Quantitative and Mixed Methods Approaches* (2nd ed, 2003)

Crotty, Michael, *The Foundations of Social Research: Meaning and Perspective in the Research Process* (Sage, 2003)

Deutsch et al, *Australian Tax Handbook 2000* (ATP, 2000)

Elliott, Jane, (Sage, 2005)

Fischer, Mary, and Treba Marsh "Biological Assets: Financial Recognition and Reporting Using US and International Accounting Guidance" (2013) 13(2) *Journal of Accounting and Finance* 57.

Fullarton, Alexander Robert, Heat, *Dust and Taxes: A Story of Tax Schemes in Australia's Outback* (Ibidem Verlag, 2014)

Fullarton, Alexander, and Dale Pinto, 'Tax Accounting for Livestock: Mother or Meat/Capital or Revenue' (2021) 27(1) *New Zealand Journal of Taxation Law and Policy* 39

Fullarton, Alexander, and Dale Pinto 'The *Wade Case*: An Analysis' (2021) 27(2) *New Zealand Journal of Taxation Law and Policy* 121

Fullarton, Alexander, and Dale Pinto 'The Foundations of the *Wade Case*: Concrete or Clay?' (2022) 24 (1) *Journal of Australian Taxation* 35

Gunn, John Angus Lancaster, and Richard Esmond O'Neill (eds), *Commonwealth Taxation Board of Review Decisions (New Series)* (Butterworth and Co, 1952) 1; (1 CTBR (NS))

Kenny, Paul, and Ken Devos *Australian Small Business Taxation* (Butterworths, 2018)

Magarey, Donald, *Buying and Selling Businesses and Companies* (Butterworths, 2nd ed, 1989)

McKerchar, Margaret, *Design and Conduct of Research in Tax, Law and Accounting* (Thomson Reuters, 2010)

Mc Nab, Paul, 'Private Rulings: Are they worth it?' (2022) 57(1) *Taxation in Australia* 38

Melbourne University Law Review *Australian Guide to Legal Citation* (4th ed, 2018).

Merriam, Sharan B, *Qualitative Research and Case Study Applications in Education* (2nd ed, Jossey-Bass, 1998)

Miles, Mathew B, and A Michael Huberman *Qualitative Data Analysis* (2nd ed, Sage, 1994)

Parker, Colin, (ed) *Accounting Handbook 2001: Volume 1 of the Accounting and Auditing Handbook 2001* (Prentice Hall, 2001)

Prebble, John, 'Intention to Make a Profit and "Business" in Section 65(2)(A) of the Income Tax Act 1976' (1978) 4 *Otago Law Review* 165.

Sims, Michele A, and Robert Charles Clift *Australian Corporate Accounting: The Formulation, Expansion and Dissolution of Companies* (McGraw-Hill, 2001) 74, 173; Craig Deegan *Financial Accounting Theory* (McGraw-Hill, 2001)

Stevenson, Angus, (ed), *Shorter Oxford English Dictionary: On Historical Principles* (6th ed, 2007)

Sydenstricker-Neto, John, "Research Design and Mixed-Method Approach: A Hands-on Experience" (1997)

Yin, Robert K, *Case Study Research: Design and Methods* (3rd ed, Sage, 2003)

Yorston, Keith, Eugene Bryan Smyth and Samuel Raymond Brown, *Advanced Accounting* (Law Book, 1978)

# B Cases

*Commissioners of Inland Revenue v Brooks* (1915) AC 478

*Commissioners of Inland Revenue v Newcastle Breweries Ltd* (1927) 12 TC 927. Reported in K.BD, 42 TLR. 185, CA., 42 TLR. 609, and H.L, *43 TLR. 476

*Commissioners of Inland Revenue v Northfleet Coal & Ballast Co* (1927) 12 TC 1102

*Commissioners of Inland Revenue v Executors of Williams* (1943) 1 All E.R. 318

*Commissioner of Taxation v Wade* (High Court of Australia, Kitto J. 4 September)

*Danmark Pty Ltd v Federal Commissioner of Taxation* (1944) 7 ATD 333

*Farnsworth v Federal Commissioner of Taxation* [1949] HCA 27; (1949) 78 CLR 504

*Federal Commissioner of Taxation v Wade ('Wade Case')* (1951) 84 CLR 105

*Kelsall Parsons & Co v Inland Revenue* [1938] SC 238

*Maritime Electric Co Ltd v General Dairies Ltd* (1937) AC 610

*McClelland v Federal Commissioner of Taxation* [1970] UKPCHCA 1; (1970) 120 CLR 487

Robinson v Federal Commissioner of Taxation [1927] HCA 8; (1927) 39 CLR 297

Short Bros., Ltd v Commissioners of Inland Revenue (1927) 12 TC 955

South Australia v Commonwealth ("First Uniform Tax case) [1942] HCA 14; 65 CLR 373 (23 July 1942)

*Stebbing v Metropolitan Board of Works* (1870) LR 6 QB 37

*he Commissioners of Inland Revenue v J Gliksten & Son, Ltd* [1929] UKHL TC 14 364 (22 February 1929)

*The Minister for Lands v Ricketson and the Australian Mortgage, Land & Finance Co* (1898) 19 LR NSW 281

Van Den Berghs, Ltd v Clark (1935) AC 431, 19 TC 390

*Wade v Commissioner of Taxation*, Commonwealth Taxation Board of Review No. 2. (1950) No M37/1950. Note: The matter is also reported as (1950) 1 CTBR (NS) Case 77, 335; and (1950) 1TBRD Case 72, 273

# C Legislation

*Acts Interpretation Act 1901* (Cth)

*Australia Act 1986* (Cth)

*Income Tax Assessment Act 1922* (Cth)

*Income Tax Assessment Act 1936* (Cth)

*Income Tax Assessment Act 1997* (Cth)

Income Tax Act 2007 (NZ),

Statute Law Revision Act 1981 (Cth)

*Tax Agent Services Act 2009* (Cth)

# D Treaties

None

# E Other

Australian Accounting Standards Board *Accounting Standards AASB 116* (2019)

Australian Accounting Standards Board *Accounting Standards AASB 141* (2019)

Australian Bureau of Statistics Cat 6350.0

Australian Government Region Map 2023

7 march 2023 https://www.agriculture.gov.au/sites/default/files/image s/aus-broadacre-zones-regions.jpg

Australian Taxation Office, *Income Tax: Definition of Livestock and Animal Embryos* (ID 2003/726, 30 July 2003)

Australian Taxation Office *Photovoltaic Solar System* (Private Ruling, Authorisation Number 1012329040193, November 2011, edited 2019).

Code of Professional Conduct *Tax Agent Services Act 2009* (Cth)

*Commissioner of Taxation v Wade* Appeal Book High Court of Australia, 9 of 1950

Commonwealth of Australia, Administrative Appeals Tribunal, 'Tribunals in Australia: Their Roles and Responsibilities' (Web Page) <https:// www.aat.gov.au/about-the-aat/engagement/speeches-and-papers /the-honourable-justice-garry-downes-am-former-pres/tribunals-in -australia-their-roles-and-responsibilities>

Commonwealth, *Royal Commission on Taxation* (1932-34) (Ferguson Royal Commission Report)

Commonwealth, *Royal Commission on Taxation* (Third Report, 12 April 1934) (Ferguson Report)

Dairy Australia Ltd, *About Dairy Australia* (2019) <https://www.dairyaust ralia.com.au/about-dairy-australia

Dairy Australia Ltd, *Best Care for Animals* (2019) < https://www.sustainabl edairyoz.com.au/best-care-for-animals#BestCareForAnimals>

Email from Client Support Team, Tax Practitioners' Board, to Alexander Fullarton, 28 November 2019

Email from Greg Walker, Service Manager, Business & Government Solutions Strategy, Customers and Culture Landgate, to Alexander Robert Fullarton, 19 December 2019

Email from Laura Baynes, Institute of Public Accountants to Alexander Fullarton, 21 October 2019.

Explanatory Memorandum, Bill for an Act to Consolidate and Amend the Income Tax Assessment Act 1922-1934, 1935

Government of Western Australia *Business Activity* (2019) <https://catalog ue.data.wa.gov.au/>.

Letter from Alison Lendon, Deputy Commissioner of Taxation, to Alexander Fullarton, 6 November 2019

New Zealand Inland Revenue Department, Tax Technical, ' Income Tax — Timing of Disposal and Derivation of Income from Trading Stock' BR PUB 14/08 (30 September 2014) <https://www.taxtechnical.ird.govt.nz /-/media/project/ir/tt/pdfs/rulings/public/pu14008.pdf?la=en>

Photograph of "Outback Heifer" taken by Alexander Robert Fullarton (2020).

Photograph of 'Meet the Crew' — the Mustering Team from De Grey Station

Tax Practitioners' Board, "Search the Register" (2019) available at <www.tpb.gov.au>

Taxation Review Committee, The Parliament of the Commonwealth of Australia, *Full Report* (Parliamentary Paper No 136, January 1975) (Asprey Report)

The Public Sector Accounting Standards Board of the Australian Accounting Research Foundation and the Australian Accounting Standards Board "Statement of Accounting Concepts SAC 4 (3/95) Definition and Recognition of the Elements of Financial Statements" (1995) available at <www.aasb.gov.au>

Transcript of Proceedings Before his Honour Mr Justice Kitto 4 September 1951 *Commissioner of Taxation v Wade*

Wolters Kluwer, CCH Australia *CCH iKnow* (online at 2 April 2022)